Hints & **A**llegations

Hints & Allegations

THE WORLD (IN POETRY AND PROSE)

ACCORDING TO

WILLIAM M. KUNSTLER

FOUR WALLS EIGHT WINDOWS
New York / London

Dedicated to my clients and comrades,

who have helped to make almost fifty years of lawyering

so much more than just a way to make a living.

A Four Walls Eight Windows First Edition

Copyright © 1994 by William M. Kunstler
Introduction copyright © 1994 by Allen Ginsberg
Printed in the United States of America

Library of Congress Cataloging-in-Publication Data
Kunstler, William Moses, 1919–

    Hints and allegations : the world, in poetry and prose, according to William M. Kunstler

    p.   cm.

    ISBN 1-56858-017-7 : $17.00

    1. United States—History—1969– —Poetry.   2. World politics—1985–1995—Poetry. 3. Political poetry, American. 4. Sonnets, American. I. Title. II. Title: HInts and allegations.
PS3561.U56H56   1994
811'.52—dc20

                    94-35203
                    CIP

1 2 3 4 5 6 7 8 9 10
Designed by Cindy LaBreacht

Contents

William Kunstler has faced the raw brutality of "Establishment" police government. He's cut to the quick like a surgeon to bare the afflicted nerve center, the nexus of significant facts, in case after case of injustice covered up by racist and/or neoconservative hypocrisy in law. This book of sonnets and prefatory commentaries is a useful history lesson for a new generation as well as for senior folk who remember outrageous cases but have forgotten the gist of evidence that made these specific legal trials and tribulations painful public scandals—injustices buried in the American subconscious—painful to recall—sorrowful to remember again—necessary to realize for our own mental health. Purification requires recognition of the negative trauma, remorse, reparation if possible, and vow of non-repetition of the injury. These sonnets and commentaries serve that end.

Though Kunstler's thinking is notoriously radical, the poetry itself is in conventional sonnets, some verses imperfect in meter, most regular footed, their information is invaluable. Coupled with prefatory commentaries, thumbnail sketches getting to the heart of evidence, this text is readable, mind-awakening—I found myself scanning through it engrossed with the historical detail:—Info on the "Primitive Man" FBI policy of investigating "without cause" black officials in Atlanta; Alcee Hastings an honest judge, persecuted; indictment and acquittal of police officer Arno Herwerth for killing Mary Mitchell; Dhoruba/Moore's ordeal of false imprisonment; set-up trial of Sgt. Clayton Lonetree, once guard at U.S. Moscow Embassy; piths of falsified evidence in Leonard Peltier's Pine Ridge shootout imprisonment trial.

And quite a few flashes of the sonneteer's wit:

Re: Chicago Conspiracy Trial:

"It matters not how fast the seasons flow

The Eight will live again on H.B.O."
Re: Larry Davis' many courtroom frame-ups:
"They fabricate each witness and each clue
To finish what their bullets failed to do."

I like William Kunstler. He's an extraordinary legal intelligence with mind that cuts through a mass of legal bullshit and media brainwash. I like his outrageous "Progressive" attitude, which boils down to a respect for truth in detail, and insistence on intimate fact. I'd bear false witness if I praised these sonnets as elegant poesy, but I must be honest and say I'm magnetized by his presentation of the underside facts of our domestic history, and succinct summary of key evidence.

Allen Ginsberg, New York, N.Y.
August, 1994

have been writing sonnets since I was a student at Yale University some fifty-three years ago. My first book of verse, *Our Pleasant Vices*, a collection of forty sonnets, twenty by me and a like number by a classmate, was published in 1940. Since then, I have written hundreds, perhaps thousands, of sonnets, usually employing the same Shakespearean rhyming scheme. In recent years, I have become the poet laureate of the Amsterdam News, a black weekly published in New York City by Wilbert Tatum, an old friend of mine, who has continually encouraged me to keep sending in my sonnets, most of which he has immortalized on his editorial page.

I like the sonnet form because it is long enough to get the message across and short enough to prevent boredom. In addition, it is an ideal vehicle to treat political subjects and make them palatable to many people. For hundreds of years, sonnets have been used to condemn militarism, war, and racism, to celebrate the lives of fighters for human rights, and to protest inhumane working and prison conditions, among other blights on civilization's escutcheon. Poets like Rupert Brooke, Dylan Thomas, Alfred, Lord Tennyson, Siegfried Sassoon, Wilfred Owen, Countee Cullen, Robert Hayden, Edna St. Vincent Millay, Robert Lowell, and Margaret Walker, to name but two handfuls, have utilized the sonnet form to expound their personal political views.

With the help of Four Walls Eight Windows, my dedicated publishers, I have selected a hundred or so of my past efforts in the hope that they stimulate readers to progressive action and other poets to use their talents to advance the paramount cause of human liberation. In any event, here are my offerings, for better or worse, presented under a title which my friend, Paul Simon, has graciously permitted me to use. The phrase "Hints and Allegations," appears in the song, "You Can Call Me Al," from Paul

Simon's "Graceland" album. In addition, I want to express my appreciation to my old friend and traveling companion, Allen Ginsberg, for consenting to write a preface to this book.

W.M.K., New York, N.Y.
September, 1994.

When Abbie Hoffman was found dead, ostensibly a suicide at the age of fifty-two, in his apartment in New Hope, Pennsylvania, on April 12, 1989, there passed from the American scene a most remarkable personality. He was an early fighter for black voting rights in Mississippi, a founder of the Youth International Party (YIP), an organizer of such unique protests as throwing dollar bills onto the floor of the New York Stock Exchange and encouraging thousands to come to Washington to "levitate" the Pentagon, and, with Jerry Rubin, the creator of the Festival of Life during the Democratic National Convention in Chicago in August of 1968. More than any other single person, he brought the concepts of music, satire, and ridicule into progressive politics. I sat with him at counsel table for six long months during the 1969-70 Chicago Conspiracy Trial when, with consummate wit and flair, he brought both the prosecutors and the judge to their figurative knees. Even when he was underground, after being charged with a sale of cocaine to an undercover agent, he remained politically active, under the symbolic name of Barry Freed, in efforts to prevent the pollution of the St. Lawrence and Delaware Rivers. The extent of his influence can be seen in the unanimous vote of the Los Angeles City Council, two days after his death, to adjourn in his memory. There will, I fear, never be one quite like him but, like so many of those who knew and loved him, it is quite impossible for me to imagine him dead and I seem to hear his New England twang everywhere. Even at his memorial service at New York's Palladium in August of 1989, there were signs reading "Abbie Lives."

He fought for People's Park in '61

    And voting rights in Mississippi, too;

He devastated Daley with a pun

    And taught his country folk to laugh on cue.

He ran a youthful pig for President

    And threw some dollars on the Market floor;

He joined the thousands in a Woodstock tent

    And raised the Pentagon a foot or more.

He tried to keep two eastern rivers clear

    And saw to it the Yippies came to be;

He didn't deviate from year to year,

    Insisting that each human must stay free.

He may be gone but I suspect he's near

    And if you listen close, his laugh you'll hear.

On November 19, 1985, a horde of New York City police officers broke into the South Bronx apartment of Regina Lewis, the sister of a black teenager, Larry Davis, whom, they later said, they merely wanted to question. Davis, who was in the apartment, fled the area after a shootout in which six officers were seriously wounded. Davis later surrendered to the FBI and was promptly charged in the Bronx with the murders of four drug dealers and the shooting of the police officers. He was also indicted for the killing of a Manhattan drug dealer. After successive Bronx juries acquitted him of all the serious charges against him in that county, the authorities kept reiterating that Bronx juries, which were usually composed of a majority of blacks and Latinos, were prejudiced against both prosecutors and the police. This assertion quickly proved to be false when a Manhattan jury, with a majority of whites, also acquitted Larry, whose Muslim name is now Adam Abdul-Hakim. Lynne Stewart and I represented him at his first two trials, and Michael (Tariffe) Warren at his third.

The Third Acquittal
of **A**dam **A**bdul-**H**akeem

FORMERLY KNOWN AS LARRY DAVIS

When Adam was acquitted in the past,

    The police said racist juries set him free,

That panels in the Bronx played loose and fast

    With all our concepts of equality.

But now another trial has taken place,

    This time down in Manhattan's lower clime,

In which a jury, split in half by race,

    Decided he was guilty of no crime.

It's fast becoming very clear indeed

    That all these charges were not based on fact

But solely on the Police Department's need

    For one dramatic and revengeful act.

They fabricate each witness and each clue

    To finish what their bullets failed to do.

Salvador Agron, the youngest person ever to be sentenced to death in New York, was convicted of fatally stabbing two members of a rival gang in a rumble in a school yard. Called "The Cape Man" because he wore a nurse's cape during the fatal confrontation, his sentence was commuted to life imprisonment by then Gov. Averill Harriman, following urgent pleas on his behalf by Eleanor Roosevelt and other influential people. He taught himself to read and write and his articles were published by *The New York Times* and other publications. He also conducted classes in English for other Spanish-speaking inmates. After serving some nineteen years, he was given the opportunity to attend college during the day, returning to prison every night. The contrast between freedom during the day and imprisonment at night was too much for him and he finally could take it no more and fled to the Southwest, where he ultimately surrendered. I represented him at his absconding trial in which we pleaded temporary insanity due to his reaction to a life that was half-free and half-custodial. He was acquitted and, after a stint in a psychiatric facility, was released. He later died of mysterious causes and I attended his wake at a Bronx funeral parlor. He was returned to his native Puerto Rico for burial.

The nurse's cape he wore that fateful day

    Had symbolized the leadership he'd won,

But later led authorities to say

    He was the youth by whom the deeds were done.

Condemned to die at sixteen years of age,

    His life was saved by those who understood

The nature and causes of his rage

    That made the bad indifferent to the good.

The years in prison wrought a startling change

    In one who seemed to have no chance at all

To then reveal an unsuspected range

    Of talents sadly now beyond recall.

His sister said that he was never free

    Until he passed into eternity.

Dhoruba, whose slave name was Richard Moore, was one of the defendants in the 1970 trial of 21 Black Panthers who were accused of a conspiracy to blow up New York department stores and other public places on Easter Sunday, 1969. After the longest criminal trial in the state's history, eight months, all of the Panthers were acquitted by their jury. Six days later, two police officers guarding Manhattan District Attorney Frank Hogan's residence were severely injured by machine gun fire. Dhoruba was arrested two weeks after the shootings and charged with the crimes, and was eventually convicted and sentenced to a prison term of 25-years to life. The single key prosecution witness was a woman named Pauline Joseph who gave extremely damaging testimony against him. Fourteen years later, it was discovered that she had made a number of earlier statements to the authorities which totally contradicted her trial testimony, none of which had ever been turned over to the defense as is required by law. Following lengthy legal proceedings, Dhoruba was released, after serving nineteen years, and, thus far, the prosecution's strenuous efforts to return him to prison have failed. As is usual when official misconduct of this magnitude is uncovered, no persons responsible for it are ever prosecuted, even when their criminality has resulted in the stripping away of so much of a man's life.

The Ordeal of
Dhoruba **Al**-**M**ujahid **B**in **W**ahad

When he survived the mammoth eight-month trial

    That failed to down the Panther 21,

The system thought that it could prove by guile

    That he ambushed two policemen with a gun.

It hid a witness from all public sight

    And worked on her for twenty months or more

Until she got her untrue story right,

    Then hid her contradictory tales galore.

They manufactured fingerprints and lied

    That he possessed the weapon in the case;

There was no dirty trick they left untried,

    To put him in a penitential place.

But truth emerged at last and now we know

    Just who the criminals were who stooped so low.

In 1987, Arizona Governor Evan Meacham repealed an executive order that declared Martin Luther King's birthday an official holiday in that state, despite the fact that the date had been designated a national holiday. In 1990, Arizona's voters defeated two propositions restoring the slain civil rights leader's birthday as a state holiday. The decisions led to a vast economic boycott, which has been estimated to have cost the state $140,000,000 in lost revenues, and caused the National Football League to withdraw the scheduled 1993 Super Bowl site from Phoenix. In November 1992, the voters reinstated King's birthday as a paid state holiday.

"**A**rizona Votes to End **K**ing Holiday"

HEADLINE, NOVEMBER 7, 1990

In Arizona now, the voters say,

    The Ides of January will not be

A time to celebrate the natal day

    Of one who symbolized equality.

It may be hard for them to understand

    That there are stellar souls who are not white

Who, in the lengthy history of this land,

    Have made a contribution just as bright.

Until there is a change in point of view,

    And Martin's birthday is at last restored,

Let's end Fiesta Bowls and tourists, too,

    To show how much their action is abhorred.

If we are firm, perhaps this Sun Belt state

    Will learn it pays a heavy price for hate.

Nora Astorga, a former corporate lawyer in Nicaragua, became a folk hero to the Sandinistas when she lured a Somozan general to her bedroom so that he could be assassinated. During the Sandinista regime, she was named her country's ambassador to the United Nations. Unfortunately, her career was shortlived because of an untreatable cancer and she died early in 1988 at the age of thirty-nine. Ironically, she was given an impressive memorial service in St. Patrick's Cathedral, the bastion of conservatism in New York, which added an air of unreality to the event. There were many of us who thought that she would have strenuously opposed this choice of church, but, once you're dead, you have no control over such matters. I like to think that her fingers were crossed during the services.

To **N**ora **A**storga

ST. PATRICK'S CATHEDRAL, FEBRUARY 23, 1989

She died, they say, because each sickly cell

    Metastasized into a thousand rife,

Until they forced the spirit from the shell

    And closed at thirty-nine this vibrant life.

And yet we know she did not really die,

    This wondrous lady of the sword and flame,

But sits upon a rebel chair on high

    And marvels that we praise her earthly fame.

For she would be the very first to say,

    We come and go like ripples on a stream,

But hope to justify our transient stay

    And add dimension to the endless dream.

This church, which plays its sad repressive role,

    Is honored by this Sandinista soul.

HINTS &
ALLEGATIONS

On Monday morning, September 13, 1971, the State Police and a horde of correction officers attacked some 1,200 rebellious inmates at the Attica Correctional Facility, a maximum security penal institution some thirty miles east of Buffalo, N.Y. Four days earlier, the prisoners had seized control of Attica's D-Yard as well as a large number of hostages. After four days of fruitless negotiations between the authorities and a committee composed of persons, including myself, requested by the inmates, Governor Nelson Rockefeller ordered that D-Yard be retaken. As a result, thirty-nine people, including a number of hostages, were shot to death. Just prior to the onslaught, I stood near the prison's front gate and watched enraged troopers and correction officers rush in, some shouting "Save me a nigger!" When the shooting stopped, an Attica spokesperson told the waiting press that the attack had been generated by the spectacle of inmates cutting the hostages' throats. This soon proved to be an utter lie as the Monroe County Coroner, who conducted the autopsies of all the dead, determined that every victim had been shot and that no one's throat had been cut. By the time D-Yard was secured, the State Police had committed unspeakable atrocities upon the surviving inmates, including making them run a gauntlet between lines of club-wielding officers.

Attica **R**emembered

Now, sixteen years have passed and I can still

    Recall the horror that I felt inside

As troopers, hungry to begin the kill,

    Pursued the plan by which so many died.

The helicopters said no one would die

    Who sought the safety of the state again,

And then the tear gas drifted from the sky

    Until the yard was filled with blinded men.

With shouts of "Save a nigger for my gun!"

    Attackers stormed onto the rebel ground

To pick off prostrate inmates, one by one,

    And torture those their weapons had not downed.

On his estate, four hundred miles away,

    The waiting Governor did not pause to pray.

Marion Barry served as a field secretary of the Student Nonviolent Coordinating Committee (SNCC) in the 1960s. He later was elected Mayor of Washington, D.C. until his conviction on drug charges in 1990. The victim of a joint FBI-DC Police sting operation, he was lured to a Washington hotel by Rasheeda Moore, a former girl friend, by promises of sex and drugs. He was arrested on January 18, 1990, and his trial took place in the summer. His jury found him guilty of only one misdemeanor possession charge, acquitted him of another, and could not reach any verdicts on the remaining twelve. His white judge, Thomas Penfield Jackson, sentenced him to a jail term of six months, a fine of $5,000.00, and one year's probation. Along with Kenneth Mundy, his trial lawyer, I argued his appeal which resulted in the vacating of his sentence on highly technical grounds. Judge Jackson, who had publicly accused Marion's jury of violating their oaths of office, quickly re-imposed the same sentences. On September 13, 1994, he won the Democratic mayoral nomination, virtually assuring reelection.

The Trial of **M**arion **B**arry

The Government decided that it was time

    To put Mayor Barry out to pasture fast,

So it arranged to stage a cocaine crime,

    Complete with former lovers in the cast.

With hidden video cameras in the wall,

    The agents taped each moment of the scene

So they could bring about their quarry's fall,

    No matter if their methods were unclean.

But juries have begun to understand

    Entrapment is quite far beyond the pale,

And when it's planned with some cop's dirty hand,

    No one should ever have to go to jail.

When our officialdom has stooped so low,

    We all must utter a resounding "No!"

I first met Harry when he opened his house to Martin Luther King for a strategy meeting just prior to the Birmingham, Alabama, protest campaign in April of 1963. Since that time, I have run into him at many demonstrations for human rights in New York and elsewhere. When Russell Means, one of the leaders of the occupation by members of the American Indian Movement (AIM) of the hamlet of Wounded Knee in February of 1973, was stabbed by a white inmate in the South Dakota Penitentiary, Harry joined Marlon Brando, Joseph Lowery of the Southern Christian Leadership Conference (SCLC), and myself at the prison in an effort to prevent any repetition of the attempt to murder Russell. This sonnet was written when Harry was presented with an award by his fellow performers for his enormous contribution to the cause of human liberty. I believe that his example played a significant role in persuading other entertainers such as Elizabeth Taylor, Ed Asner, Susan Sarandon, Tim Robbins, Danny Glover, Val Kilmer, and Robert De Niro, to name but seven, to stand up and be counted.

Harry **B**elafonte

The songs he sang came from a culture's past

    And brought to life an island's melody,

With words that made the gossip travel fast

    To every corner of society.

An entertainer, yes, but one with skill

    To use his talent to proclaim the true—

That none should starve while others ate their fill,

    And Indians deserve their treaties' due.

He sang to curb discrimination's blight

    And gave himself, his home and ready cash

In furtherance of every southern fight

    To end the remnants of the bondsman's lash.

He proved that those who live to entertain

    Must also help to fracture every chain.

In late 1970, I spent three hours with Harry Blackmun on a plane between Dallas, Texas, and Phoenix, Arizona. He approached me shortly after we were in the air and asked whether he could sit with me. During the flight, we discussed everything under the sun and I recall telling him that being called a Minnesota Twin because of his association with Chief Justice Warren E. Burger was no way to go down in history. When we landed in Phoenix, where he was scheduled to address a conference of state judges, we embraced and he went his way and I mine. Later, I was flattered to read in Bob Woodward's book about the Supreme Court, *The Brethren*, that he had told his law clerks, upon his return to Washington, that he had been mighty pleased to have been hugged by a "radical lawyer." His metamorphosis from a mousy moderate to a fighter for decency and morality in the legal sphere is as inspirational as it was unexpected.

On the Retirement of
Justice Harry Blackmun

He first was called a Minnesota Twin

    Because, like Burger, he came from that state,

But later gave the Court his unique spin

    And soon was writing on a different slate.

I like to think I played a tiny role

    In pushing him away from Rehnquist's blight

Until the pressures of his liberal soul

    Began to end the mayhem of the right.

He penned the words that saved a woman's choice

    To legally abort her pregnancy;

His was the lonely but enlightened voice

    That punishment by death should never be.

There's little that we owe to Nixon's reign,

    But naming Harry may reduce the stain.

When then United States Attorney Rudolph Giuliani was preparing his prosecution of New York's so-called leading Organized Crime Families, known as the Commission Case, he subpoenaed Joe "Joe Bananas" Bonanno, then living with a daughter in Tucson, Arizona, to give a videotaped deposition in September 1985 as an expert on organized crime. He stated that he intended to question Bonanno about material appearing in the latter's autobiography, "A Man of Honor," published two years earlier. Bonanno, who was thought to be the former head of the Family that bore his name, was in his eighties and suffering from high blood pressure and a narrowing of the arteries. Nevertheless, Giuliani insisted that the subpoena be enforced, and the trial judge, Richard Owen, a strong pro-government jurist, ordered that a hearing be held in Tucson with reference to the state of Bonanno's health. I was asked by Charles R. Garry, Bonanno's regular attorney, who was then on trial in San Francisco, to represent his client. The prosecution team, the defense lawyers, and the judge all traveled to Tucson where the hearing was held in a local hospital's lecture hall. Despite convincing testimony from Bonanno's physicians as to the dangers to their patient's health if he was required to obey the subpoena, Owen, quite predictably, ordered him to give the deposition in question. When I vigorously protested, the judge threatened to hold me in contempt. Of course, Giuliani & Company knew that Bonanno would go to jail rather than testify and the attempt to subpoena him was nothing more than a cheap publicity stunt. Predictably, Bonanno refused to honor the subpoena and was found guilty of civil contempt and served nearly fourteen months at the United States Medical Center in Springfield, Missouri. A month after his release, he was indicted for criminal contempt, but the charges were dropped when it was determined that he was suffering from incurable "senile dementia."

The old man limped into the lecture hall

    And sank into a chair set near the door;

His doctors waited for a distress call

    While news reporters scanned their monitor.

Just as the witness sighed a low-pitched groan,

    The judge, in robes that seemed quite out of place,

Swept, like a monarch, to his makeshift throne,

    A beatific smile upon his face.

The prosecutor, with a knowing look,

    Strode to the fore, impatient to be heard,

To start the questioning from his quarry's book,

    Alone concerned the press got every word.

You hardly need the wisdom of the ages

    To know some things should not be put on pages.

In late 1956, I was asked by the American Civil Liberties Union in 1956 to represent William Worthy, Jr., a black reporter for CBS, who had dared to travel to what was then referred to as "Red" China, a country ruled off-limits for Americans, and whose passport had been confiscated because of his trip. I knew absolutely nothing about this aspect of the law, so I turned to Leonard Boudin who, for years, had been fighting the State Department over its restrictive travel policy. He was most gracious in assisting me in drawing up a federal complaint on Worthy's behalf, and I obtained the services of Edward Bennett Williams, then a young Washington, D.C. practitioner, to serve as local counsel. Although we did not win, I learned a great deal from Leonard who became a lifelong friend and advisor. His many appearances before the Supreme Court were legendary and he was one of the great amateur chess players of our time. When he died in 1989, the progressive bar lost one of its greatest champions.

To **L**eonard **B**oudin

The country's filled with lawyers everywhere

    Who, for a fee, would fight the Devil's cause,

And do not demonstrate the slightest care

    What villainies are hidden by the laws.

Yet, there are those who have a different sense

    Of what a lawyer's role in life should be,

Whose souls are never slaves to pounds or pence

    But only to a moral currency.

Our Leonard's drumbeat was not hard to hear,

    A rat-a-tat that led him toward the skies

That lightened as this hopeful man drew near

    To where not gold but people were the prize.

Upon the list of those who've met the test,

    You'll find our fallen friend leads all the rest.

When Saddam Hussein invaded oil-rich Kuwait in the late summer of 1990, President Bush seized upon the incident to bolster his declining popularity in the face of a rapidly deepening recession. He threatened to use military force if the Iraqi leader did not withdraw and persuaded the United Nations to rubber stamp his hard line. Finally, in January of 1991, American planes, using the latest bombing equipment and techniques, began what was to be a month of round the clock attacks on Baghdad, sorties which levelled many civilian structures as well as military ones. The air raids were followed by an invasion of Iraq by hundreds of thousands, mainly American, who succeeded in killing untold numbers of the Iraqi defenders. When hostilities ceased, the Emir of Kuwait, who had sat out the war in luxurious European hotels, returned to his fiefdom. From the beginning, there was little doubt that the so-called Gulf War had nothing to do with morality but only with the price of gasoline.

Hail **C**aesar

We who are soon to die salute you now,

    Our noble President who threatens force

So that Saddam Hussein will finally cow

    And terminate the controversy's source.

He tells us that one man can stop the fray,

    By that he means the leader of Iraq,

But we know that he, too, can utter nay

    Before there is no final turning back.

For those who fall upon the desert soil,

    The telegrams will publicize our fate;

We gave our all for barrels filled with oil

    And to restore the Emir of Kuwait.

Come now, let's beat the new Pied Piper's drum—

    We're off to fight for Gulf Petroleum!

In the spring of 1968, led by Daniel and Philip Berrigan, Roman Catholic priests, nine anti-war activists, seven men and two women, entered a draft board in Catonsville, a Baltimore suburb, seized 500 1-A files, and burned them with homemade napalm in the street. They were promptly arrested and charged with destroying government property above the value of $100.00, a federal felony. Along with a number of other lawyers, I represented them at their trial which provided some of the most moving courtroom scenes I have ever experienced. The testimony of the defendants as to just why they were willing to risk their liberty in order to try and stop the killing in Vietnam was as eloquent as it was inspirational. When Daniel Berrigan finished his explanation, he asked the judge whether he could lead the courtroom in the Lord's Prayer. The judge turned to the United States Attorney for his reaction to this unorthodox request, to which the latter, to his eternal credit, replied, "The government not only assents, but will join in the recitation." With that, Dan began to intone the familiar words of the prayer as spectators held up lit candles. Although the jury convicted them all, the Catonsville Nine, as they came to be called, had set an example for the entire country. For example, a group known as the Milwaukee Fourteen soon emulated them in that Wisconsin city. In 1993, I joined most of the defendants in a reunion at a Baltimore college where we relived those marvelous days of twenty-five years ago.

Catonsville—
Twenty-Five Years Later

1968-1993

A quarter of a century ago,

> The Nine decided that it was high time

To dramatize just what we all know—

> We were engaged in genocidal crime.

They burned with homemade napalm 1-A files

> And may have saved 500 youthful souls,

Then tried to illustrate at later trials

> That, after all, morality controls.

And yet we realize that, since those days,

> In Panama, Grenada, and the rest,

Our country still has never learned the ways

> To ape our loving friends' so heartfelt quest.

Let's make our memories of Catonsville

> Remind us that its goal is needed still.

In the early morning hours of December 20, 1989, President Bush ordered an invasion of Panama by 20,000 American troops in a thinly disguised attempt to find General Manuel Antonio Noriega, that country's chief executive, and bring him back to the United States for trial. The paradox between this country's tolerance of Paraguay's General Alfredo Stroessner, Nicaragua's Anastasio Somoza, and Iran's Shah, and its vendetta against Noriega, who was for many years on the CIA payroll, is amazing, to put it mildly. General Noriega was captured, following a long hunt for him, and then brought to Miami, Florida, where he ultimately went on trial, on a federal indictment containing many racketeering and drug counts. Although the trial judge recognized Noriega's status as a prisoner of war, he was convicted, and sentenced to a prison term of forty years, which he is presently serving at the Metropolitan Correctional Center, Homestead, Florida. Just before his trial began, his secretary was subpoenaed to appear as a witness for the prosecution. I represented her in her successful efforts to avoid testifying against her former employer. Recently, I received a copy of the general's appellate brief, along with a letter from him asking me to consider submitting a friend of the court brief on his behalf. If time permits, I certainly will do so.

Christmas Time in Panama

The President wants Noriega dead

    And so he sends in 20,000 men

And puts a dollar bounty on his head

    So he will never bother him again.

We hardly tried to pull the late Shah's pins

    Or terminate apartheid's awful sway;

We co-existed with Somoza's sins

    And had no fault to find with Paraguay.

Our public purpose is to extradite

    One man to face a federal court down south,

But is it worth this lethal show of might

    And can we trust the Presidential mouth?

There must be something that the general knows

    That terrifies our George from head to toes.

In 1985, the city of Philadelphia, Pennsylvania, had its first black mayor, Wilson Goode, a former client of mine. In order to evict the members of MOVE, a small group of very militant blacks, all of whom had adopted the surname of Africa, Mayor Goode authorized the dropping of a powerful incendiary bomb upon their house. This resulted in the incineration of eleven occupants of the MOVE house, including infants, and the destruction of some sixty dwellings in the immediate vicinity. At first, the city officials lied about the nature of the bomb but eventually its high explosive makeup was disclosed, resulting in the resignation of the city's Chief of Police. I filed a petition on behalf of the MOVE survivors seeking the indictment of the mayor and a number of involved public officials, but it was eventually dismissed. Later, the city was forced to rebuild the destroyed residences and pay a substantial sum to the heirs of the MOVE victims.

The City of **B**rotherly **L**ove

The neighbors had complained that MOVE was odd

    And that its dogs would bark, day out and in,

That garbage filled the corners of its sod

    While amplifiers pierced the air with din.

The city's fathers thought the time had come

    To evict this strange and strident band;

So they prepared a large explosive bomb

    And threw it from a state-owned plane as planned.

The thing was dropped without a warning sound

    And turned the house into a funeral pyre;

The flames burned sixty houses to the ground

    And exorcised eleven lives by fire.

The murderers then lied about the raid

    Because they knew no piper would be paid.

The late Eugene "Bull" Connor, who died of cancer of the mouth some years ago, was, as Birmingham's Commissioner of Public Safety during the 1960s, the architect of that city's "get tough" policy for demonstrators against segregation. When he ordered his minions to use attack dogs and fire hoses against even children, the sight of such brutality on the evening television news did more to end overt discrimination in Birmingham than any other single factor. In fact, one of the firemen, when directed by Connor to hose a group of young demonstrators, became so disgusted with what he was asked to do that he refused to follow the Commissioner's order. When the demonstrators learned of this, they redoubled their efforts to bring the authorities to the negotiation table.

Bull **C**onnor
Lives Once More

1989

So many souls have gone into the dust

    To gain the object of a freedom quest

And warn the power structure that it must

    Provide a break for those so long oppressed.

First Medgar, Malcolm X, and Martin, too,

    Gave up their lives to push for human rights,

While thousands marched down every avenue

    To force morality to greater heights.

In time, the nation found a ready way

    Affirmatively to correct the past,

Till Reagan ushered in a darker day

    By naming judges sworn to go back fast.

What segregationists can do no more,

    The high court does by votes of five to four.

A few days after Christmas, 1990, an evening rap concert was scheduled at the gymnasium of New York's City College. So many fans showed up at the building's one open door that a great deal of pushing and shoving started. It soon got out of hand and, despite pleas from the promoters, the police refused to intervene. Soon, the crowd began to surge through the entrance in such numbers that nine people were crushed to death in the resulting stampede. One white police officer, who was watching the virtually all-black audience later said that, as far as he was concerned, its members were "animals."

Death at **C**ity **C**ollege

The crowd began to gather after four,

   So eager to attend the rappers' game;

It soon had swelled to several thousand more,

   Lured by the many players' worldwide fame.

The organizer asked the police to yell

   That those without a ticket had no role;

Instead, the officers refused to tell

   And let the people grow beyond control.

At last, the fatal push was underway

   As hundreds down the narrow stairs did run;

The uniforms stood by as death held sway

   And murdered nine whose lives had just begun.

One cop who watched the blacks outside the gym,

   Said they were only "animals" to him.

In 1969-70, The Chicago Eight, composed of Tom Hayden, John Froines, Abbie Hoffman, Jerry Rubin, Dave Dellinger, Lee Weiner, Rennie Davis, and the Black Panther Chairman, Bobby Seale, were tried for their actions during the tumultuous 1968 Democratic Convention in the Windy City. During their six-month trial, the Eight (later reduced to Seven when Seale was severed because of his vociferous insistence on being represented by Charles Garry, his attorney of choice) fought every attempt of the prosecution and its blatant ally, Judge Julius Jennings Hoffman, to paint them as "evil men." They fully exposed the culpability of Mayor Richard Daley, who ordered his police to brutalize the demonstrators, who had come to Chicago to protest the war in Vietnam and racism at home. The defendants were acquitted of the most serious charge against them and the convictions obtained by the prosecution were later reversed on appeal. In 1987, Home Box Office presented a feature memorializing one of the most unusual trials in American history.

They fought the government with nail and tooth

And risked contempt to let the country see

Just what was false, just what was patent truth,

And just how rank was our hypocrisy.

They ridiculed the customs of the court

And showed it less than holier than thou;

They brought the prosecution team up short

And decimated every sacred cow.

They carefully exposed Mayor Daley's way

Of meeting protest with a billy club

To break the heads of those who came to say

The war in Viet Nam was still the rub.

It matters not how fast the seasons flow,

The Eight will live again on HBO.

HINTS &
ALLEGATIONS

47

In 1991, after a New York jury had acquitted my client, El-Sayyid Nosair of the murder of Rabbi Meir Kahane, Prof. Alan Dershowitz of the Harvard University Law School proclaimed publicly that my defense of the accused assassin was "laughably amateurish." I could easily understand such a criticism if Nosair had been convicted, but it did not seem rational in light of the jury's verdict.

A Sonnet to Commemorate Professor **A**lan **D**ershowitz's Comments

THAT THE DEFENSE WHICH RESULTED IN THE ACQUITTAL OF EL SAYYID NOSAIR
OF THE MURDER OF RABBI MEIR KAHANE WAS "LAUGHABLY AMATEURISH"

After the jury made it crystal clear

    That El Sayyid of murder guilt was free,

The press sought out the Harvard Law School seer

    To comment on this legal victory.

The dean of self-promoters promptly said,

    Although he'd never tried a jury case,

The victor's lawyers were too wrongly led

    And that their strategy was way off-base.

It is one thing to criticize a loss

    But to condemn a win is strange indeed;

Perhaps it's jealousy that won the toss

    And he was driven by a psychic need.

If he had won, it's surely safe to say,

    He would have claimed that chutzpah won the day.

In 1992, the country celebrated the "discovery" of America by Christopher Columbus. However, Native Americans, who were here centuries before Columbus ever set sail in 1492, regarded his coming to these shores as hardly a "discovery," but the beginning of the enslavement of indigenous people by the Conquistadors who followed him to what was euphemistically referred to as the New World by the Spanish and the successive waves of European predators who despoiled both the Northern and Southern Hemispheres.

The "Discovery" of **A**merica

Old Christopher Columbus found a land

    That ever was where it's supposed to be

And peopled by its own indigenous band

    Of human beings who were living free.

He was the first of pirates from the West

    Whose greed for gold grew more each passing day,

And when they'd emptied every treasure chest,

    They then enslaved or killed their native prey.

With sword and cross, they managed to despoil

    The customs of all those they'd stolen blind,

And made them spend their lives in unpaid toil

    To build their churches and their bullion find.

It makes no earthly sense to celebrate

    A trip that led to centuries of hate.

In 1987, the Supreme Court's anti-libertarian majority refused to set aside the death penalty of a Georgia black man who had been found guilty of the murder of a white victim. What was unusual about the decision was that the Court accepted the statistics compiled by an Iowa professor that a capital defendant whose victim was white stood an 80% greater chance to be sentenced to death than one who had killed someone of a different race. In other words, in America a white life was felt to be worth far more than a non-Caucasian one.

Discrimination in **D**eath

The figures fully proved the victim's skin

    Determined who would live and who would die,

That surely, if a white man was done in,

    His murderer would then be hanged on high.

But, on the other hand, if blacks were killed,

    The likelihood of death was four times less,

Insuring that the prisons would be filled

    By those whose weapons made the safer guess.

The Court's majority just closed its eyes

    To all these sentencing disparities,

Concluding that they came as no surprise

    But were the system's natural vagaries.

We've given history an awful wrench—

    The lynch mob sits now on the highest bench.

Throughout my long association with various progressive movements in the United States, I have been appalled at the individual and official violence exercised against those whose only sin was to raise their voices against racial and sexual discrimination, militarism, environmental pollution, and other perceived evils. I have witnessed the bombing and firing of black churches, the murders of civil rights workers, the use of billy clubs, dogs, and fire hoses against peaceful demonstrators, and the perversion of the law to inhibit protest marchers. To be a dissident in this society means that you have to anticipate that you may be in grave danger. Yet, the struggle for human rights must never cease, no matter how perilous it proves to be. Otherwise, freedom may well disappear for us and those who come after us.

The **D**issidents

They shoot us dead in droves or one by one

    In Carolina and the Philippines;

They execute our leaders with the gun

    Or fire it to massacre our teens.

They hang us from the branches of their trees,

    They break our heads and bones with billy sticks;

They hose us when we're praying on our knees

    And try to still our voice with dirty tricks.

They stone and burn our houses to the ground,

    They dynamite the churches where we meet;

They use the courts to bring our pennants down

    And prison walls to stay our marching feet.

If you don't want to rot or perish young,

    It may be safer still to hold your tongue.

Robert Nelson Drew was executed by lethal injection in Huntsville, Texas, a few minutes after midnight on August 2, 1994. Along with my partner, Ronald L. Kuby, I had represented Bobby for some eleven years. He was convicted on December 9, 1983, of the capital murder of Jeffrey Mays, a runaway Alabama teenager, with whom he had hitched a ride to Houston in February of that year. Some three months after his sentence was imposed, the real murderer, who had pled guilty to the crime in return for a prison term of 60 years, executed an affidavit in which he fully exonerated Drew. Later on, the key witness against our client recanted his testimony and now stated that he had not seen Bobby involved in the stabbing of Mays. However, because Texas had a rule that new evidence could not be passed upon by any court unless it was discovered within thirty days of an accused's sentencing, Drew was never given an the opportunity to move to have his conviction set aside. The Supreme Court's conservative majority refused to intervene, holding that "innocence was irrelevant." Ironically, the judge who signed his next to last execution order followed his signature with the traditional "happy face." Undoubtedly, he was reflecting the attitude of Rehnquist & Company.

Robert **N**elson **D**rew

It seems that Bobby Drew may finally die,

    A lethal needle throbbing in his vein,

And Texas then will heave a thankful sigh

    That one more human life is down the drain.

No matter that the murderer confessed

    That he alone was guilty of the crime,

Or that a crucial witness has professed

    That at the trial he lied most of the time.

In Washington, the highest court has said

    That proof of innocence can play no role,

Unless by thirty days it rears its head

    To save a much more fortunate soul.

The joyous judge, suffused with Christian grace,

    Adorned his order with a happy face.

When George Bush, during the 1988 Presidential Campaign, claimed that Michael Dukakis, his Democratic opponent, had released William Horton (referred to for obvious reasons as "Willie"), a black convict on parole, he convinced many voters that the Massachusetts Governor was "soft on crime." In Louisiana, David Duke, a former American Nazi, utilized the same scare tactics to advance his own political career. Although he succeeded in obtaining a sizeable vote in that state's gubernatorial primary, he could not keep up the momentum and, fortunately, eventually faded from the scene. When I spoke at Tulane University in 1970, Duke, wearing his Brown Shirt uniform, complete with swastika armband, paraded outside the auditorium with a sign which read: KUNSTLER, COMMUNIST JEW.

The **D**uke that **B**ush Crowned

The President used Willie Horton's name

　　To make sure that the voters understood

The subtle nature of his racist game

　　But would not think he wore a Klansman's hood.

He pandered to the white majority

　　While claiming he upheld the rights of all,

Ignoring that his hidden bigotry

　　Would cause a David Duke to heed his call.

He didn't care what strains of hate he'd bred

　　To give his Presidential hopes a boost;

He should remember what one prophet said—

　　The chickens will one day come home to roost.

Down in the bayou land, his words came clear—

　　One can advance by raising racial fear.

Eastern District High School, located in the Williamsburg area of Brooklyn, has a predominantly black student body. On October 3, 1989, a white social studies teacher delivered what many of the students considered to be a racist speech in which he belittled the black inhabitants of South Africa and praised the white rulers of that country. His remarks triggered a rampage of black and Latino students through the halls, resulting in a number of arrests and the temporary closing of the school.

Eastern District High School

The Third World pupils now at Eastern High

    Were shocked to hear a teacher who was white

State that the blacks in Africa don't try

    Or lacked the needed brains to see the light.

He claimed that when the whites were in control,

    They knew much better how to run the show,

And that, if well-run countries were the goal,

    Pretoria had shown the way to go.

Perhaps if this had been another day,

    The students never would have known a choice,

But now, insisting that they have their say,

    They let the city hear their fury's voice.

It's clear that educators must take care

    That what they teach in class be wholly fair.

Recently, it was disclosed that the leading cause of death for young black males in this country is homicide. This sonnet was written with the murders of ten such victims in mind, murders for which no one was ever convicted. The sole woman, Eleanor Bumpurs, was included because of the shocking manner in which this mentally disturbed grandmother was gunned to death in her apartment by a police officer, an episode which is the subject of another poem in this collection.

To Randy Evans, Clifford Glover, Willie Turks,

...ELEANOR BUMPURS, MICHAEL GRIFFITH, MICHAEL STEWART, NICHOLAS BARTLETT, DARYL DODSON, DARREL CABEY, EDMUND PERRY, ARTHUR MILLER—AND ALL THE OTHERS

They're choked to death on Brooklyn's busy lanes

Or underneath Manhattan's soaring domes;

They're paralyzed on speeding subway trains

Or blown to bits inside their project homes.

They're executed on a Harlem street

Or on a park path with a .38;

They're stungunned in a precinct's backroom suite

Or brutalized by mobs convulsed with hate.

It matters not that they're but nine years old,

Or honor students at a fancy school;

They're all the same to killers who are told

That amnesty for murderers is the rule.

Throughout the inner city's sprawling breadth,

Just being black remains a cause of death.

HINTS &
ALLEGATIONS

It was not until 1947 that a black managed to break into major league baseball. Branch Rickey, then general manager of the Brooklyn Dodgers, ruptured the pastime's color line when he signed Jackie Robinson to a contract. Since that time, many black players have made it to the big show, with some, like Bob Gibson, Ernie Banks, and Willie Mays, surely destined for the sport's Hall of Fame. However, most of the front offices have remained lily-white and there are still very few black field managers. However, on August 3, 1994, Northeastern University's Center for the Study of Sport in Society issued its annual report on race relations and hiring practices in various professional sports and upped Major League Baseball's grade from a "C" last year to a "B."

The **F**oulest **B**all

For years, the majors ran an all-white game,

    With blacks excluded from the national sport,

Allowed to seek their segregated fame

    In leagues where days were long and salaries short.

Then Jackie came to break the color line

    That had endured a century or more,

And paved the way for all the rest to shine,

    Bob Gibson, Ernie Banks and Mays galore.

Today, there is another bar to yield,

    Front offices are still close to lily-white,

And blacks are only good enough to field

    Or steal a base or show their batting might.

When will the owners understand at last

    That Rickey's Revolution is not past.

Following the passage of the Voting Rights Act of 1965, so many blacks were elected to public office that it resembled the Reconstruction period following the Civil War. However, it soon became clear that, just as at the end of Reconstruction in 1876, blacks were again being excluded from the political scene. Despite the fact that blacks held only 2% of all elective and appointive positions in the country, they comprised 40% of those indicted for crimes committed while in office. This disparity was partially explained by the release several years ago of an affidavit by an Atlanta lawyer who had worked for the FBI in that city in which he explained that the Bureau had a program to investigate without cause certain black Atlanta officials, on the ground that blacks lacked the capacity to hold important public positions. This program was entitled "Frühmenschen," a German word meaning "primitive man." One Pennsylvania Member of Congress, William Gray, who endured such an undemocratic tactic, refused to return to his seat and became the Director of the United Negro College Fund instead.

Frühmenschen

The FBI has made a master plan

    To label blacks who may in office sit;

It's called the German word for early man

    And is designed to prove they are unfit.

The tactic is the same that once was used

    To end the gains the Civil War had brought

And drive from power those it then abused

    By falsely claiming they were less than naught.

Today, the Bureau manufactures plots

    Designed to nullify the hard-won votes

By painting those in Harlem or in Watts

    As druggies, thieves, or bedroom goats.

It tried it once with Martin Luther King,

    And now its net is ever widening.

It has now become quite routine for prosecutors, the country over, to announce the institution of criminal charges in high publicity cases in dramatic press conferences, designed to thoroughly taint the local jury pools. As soon as they have seen to it that the print and electronic media are thoroughly saturated with their versions of the accused's culpability, they then often run to court and seek orders restraining defense counsel from responding in kind. Known as gag rules, their violation can result in jail sentences and/or fines for the attorneys who dare to attempt to counter the prosecutions' broadsides. The growing practice of muzzling criminal defense lawyers recently moved the American Bar Association to recommend that the Disciplinary Rules relating to attorneys' public statements be amended to permit them to fight fire with fire.

Gag **R**ule

The prosecutor called the willing press

    To tell just how the police had solved the case,

And that Detective Jones' enlightened guess

    Had saved them from a fruitless wild goose chase.

As soon as everyone in town had heard

    Of the official version of the crime,

The prosecutor urged the court that not a word

    Should reach the news at any future time.

The judge agreed and ordered all involved

    To stay away from television lights,

Contending that his ruling had evolved

    In order to protect the suspect's rights.

Now that the horse had left the barnyard gate,

    It would be closed, but just a trifle late.

Charles R. Garry, a California lawyer, became best known for his defense of Huey P. Newton and Bobby Seale, co-founders of the Black Panther Party. When the government indicted eight activists in early 1969 for their alleged crimes at the Democratic National Convention in Chicago the preceding summer, Charlie was selected as chief counsel with Leonard Weinglass and I as his associates. Unfortunately, he required gall bladder surgery just before the trial began and Judge Julius Hoffman refused to grant a two-week adjournment so that he could convalesce sufficiently to try the case. He often described himself as a street battler in the courtroom and taught generations of progressive lawyers, including myself, how to stand up to judicial tyranny. When he collapsed from a sudden stroke, he was rushed to a local hospital in an ambulance. During the ride, one of the medics attending him asked, "Do you have a headache?" Charlie's last words were, "I don't have headaches, I give them."

Charles Garry

This ancient warrior from the Western shore,

    Armenia's gift to our own native scene,

Who's proved his worth in legal tiffs galore

    From California to New Haven's Green;

This is the man whom we extol tonight,

    A battler in the courts of everywhere,

Who knows that truth is mightier than might

    And justice still as needed as the air.

He used to stand upon his head to clear

    The cobwebs from his teeming brain,

But right end up or right end down, no fear,

    Our Charlie knows just how to break a chain.

From Daly City to the eastern coast,

    His ardent fans make up a mammoth host.

I have always been a baseball fan, probably stemming from the days when my grandfather was one of the physicians for the New York Giants in the twenties. When that team deserted New York for San Francisco, an act I considered to be one of sheer treachery, I managed, with a great deal of effort, to transfer my loyalties to the New York Mets. However, one day in July 1989, after I had watched the team lose a doubleheader to the Houston Astros, I wrote this sonnet and sent it to Jay Horowitz, the Mets' public relations director, with the message, "In hopes this will stimulate the lads or angers them enough to react affirmatively." I don't know what happened to it after it arrived, but I did get two anonymous calls from males roundly condemning me for writing it. Like so many other fans, I have become disenchanted with the fact that the game has become, both for the owners and the players, just a vehicle to make big money.

Get **M**et—**I**t **P**ays

WITH APOLOGIES TO HOWARD JOHNSON

They talk about how much they owe their fans

    While concentrating on their bank accounts;

They work upon their early season tans

    And calculate their worth in dollar amounts.

Their bosses, too, commercialize their zeal

    By selling all that will a logo hold,

And turning what was once a sporting deal

    Into a daily hunt for increased gold.

The players, quite infected by the lure

    Of loads of shekels to be quickly made,

Are willing boos and catcalls to endure

    Provided that they are so richly paid.

They wind up on the wrong side of the score

    Because they are not hungry anymore.

I. Leo Glasser, a former Dean of the Brooklyn Law School, was appointed to the federal court in that borough by President Reagan. Many of us in the progressive bar applauded his selection because we felt that he was a liberal who could be counted on to remain on during his judicial tenure. Unfortunately, he has turned out to be just the opposite. Among other things, he permitted a number of white revolutionaries to be stungunned by marshals in his courtroom and prevented John Gotti and his co-defendant from having their attorneys of choice represent them in a trial which resulted in life imprisonment for both men. He then insisted on proffering contempt charges against one of the disqualified attorneys, Bruce Cutler, for innocuous remarks made by him to the press. His dislike of aggressive defense lawyers was manifested in one case when, after the trial, he ordered their names stricken from the list of attorneys eligible to represent indigent federal defendants.

I. Leo Glasser

"I love the law," the judge proclaims with heat,

    And then proceeds to violate its terms

By marching to the prosecution's beat

    And burying the cases with the worms.

He agonizes all throughout the trial,

    His anguish part of his Hebraic birth;

He cannot bring himself to show a smile

    Or any other evidence of mirth.

He lets the marshals beat defendants down

    And later stunned them with electric shock;

He wears upon his face a ready frown

    When he observes the prisoners in the dock.

The government selects its courts with care

    Lest one good judge should strip the system bare.

A few days before Christmas in 1985, Bernhard Goetz, a white man, using an illegal handgun, shot four black youths on a New York subway train, claiming that they were about to mug him. One of those he gunned down, Darrell Cabey, was paralyzed for life by a shot that severed his spine. Later, during a deposition in a civil case brought by me on behalf of Cabey, Goetz admitted that, after he had fired once at the youth, he said, "you don't look so bad," and shot him again. Goetz, who quickly became known as "the Subway Vigilante," was eventually acquitted of four counts of attempted murder but found guilty of the criminal possession of a weapon and served a few months in prison.

The Trial of **B**ernhard **G**oetz

The trial begins of Bernhard Hugo Goetz,

    The vigilante of the IRT,

Who, stimulated by imagined threats,

    Let bullets raise him from obscurity.

A senator announced his firm support,

    In haste before he learned of all the facts,

And vowed that he would testify in court

    In favor of the would-be murderer's acts.

No moment that, his victims on the floor,

    He looked at one and said, "You seem too fine,"

And pressed his trigger finger just once more

    To fire the shot that sliced a young man's spine.

It would be viewed in quite a different light

    If he were black and all his quarry white.

In 1989, I argued the case of Texas v. Johnson in the United States Supreme Court. Five years earlier, Johnson had, as a protest against Ronald Reagan and his policies, burned an American flag outside of the amphitheater in Dallas, Texas, where the Republican Party was preparing to nominate the President for a second term. Convicted under a Texas statute that made it a crime to burn "venerated objects," Johnson was sentenced to both a jail term and a fine. His conviction was reversed by a state appellate court but Texas persuaded the Supreme Court to review the case. After the high court's action, I received a telegram from Johnson asking me to represent him at oral argument. In a close 5-4 decision, authored by Justice William J. Brennan, the Supreme Court held that burning an American flag as a protest was protected speech under the First Amendment. An infuriated Congress immediately passed a statute making it a federal crime to burn a flag. Happily, after two lower federal courts, one in Seattle and the other in Washington, D.C., where test burnings had taken place, found the new law unconstitutional, the Supreme Court, again by a 5-4 vote, followed suit.

Goodbye, **F**reedom of **S**peech

The Court held that it was no criminal act

    To burn a flag to point out wrong from right

Or demonstrate that there were those who lacked

    A place for them to go to sleep at night.

The President, convulsed with fervent zeal,

    Sought mightily to kill the Bill of Rights

So that the Freedom Bell would cease to peal

    And turn our days into the darkest nights.

The Congress, eager to join in the game,

    But yet afraid to change the bottom line,

Responded with a statute that they name

    The Flag Protection Act of '89.

The Founding Fathers' ghosts have sadly learned

    It was the First Amendment that was burned.

On March 10, 1993, Dr. David Gunn, a gynecologist at the Pensacola, Florida, Women's Medical Services abortion clinic, was fatally shot three times in the back by Michael F. Griffin, a 32-year-old former chemical plant worker, during an Operation Rescue America demonstration. Prior to the shooting, circulars labelling the physician a murderer were posted throughout the Pensacola area. On March 6, 1994, Griffin was convicted by a jury of seven women and five men and immediately sentenced to life imprisonment. On Friday morning, July 29, 1994, Paul Hill, one of the most visible supporters at his trial who also had picketed at Dr. Gunn's funeral, gunned down gynecologist Dr. John Bayard Britton and a volunteer patient escort outside another Pensacola abortion clinic. As he was led away by police, Hill, with a broad smile on his face, said, "There will not be any more baby killings at this clinic today."

The Murder of **D**avid **G**unn

For years, the gynecologist had sought

    To stop unwarranted pregnancies galore

For any woman to his clinic brought

    Who asked his help to be with child no more.

When Operation Rescue came his way,

    It first used pickets all around his place,

Who soon blocked walks and entrances each day

    So that his patients could not seek his grace.

Then circulars were posted far and wide

    That labeled him a murderer and worse;

They made a man of unsound mind decide

    To rid the world of such an obscene curse.

Obsessed so much on saving fetal souls,

    He filled the doctor's back with bullet holes.

David Hampton, who came to New York from his home town of Buffalo in the early eighties to make it in the theater, found the going tough indeed. When he became desperate, he began to find suitable lodging by pretending to be Sidney Poitier's son. He proved to be a consummate actor who could make people believe every word he said. On one occasion, he burst into the home of Osborn Elliot, then the Dean of the Columbia School of Journalism, and said that he was a friend of Elliot's children and had just been mugged nearby. Believing that he was Poitier's son who might get them small parts in a movie his father was supposedly directing, Elliot willingly gave him bed and board. When he discovered that he'd been conned, Elliot notified the police, resulting in Hampton's conviction of fraud and a two-year jail sentence. While he was incarcerated, Elliot recounted the episode to John Guare, a friend of his, who decided to write a play about the incident. Entitled, "Six Degrees of Separation," the play became a smash hit, and eventually a feature motion picture. Hampton, as destitute as ever, contacted Guare and asked for a small share of the fortune he'd made from his story. Guare refused and persuaded Robert Morganthau, the New York County District Attorney, to charge him with making two threatening telephone calls. Along with Ron Kuby, I represented Hampton at this trial which resulted in an acquittal on one charge and a hung jury on the other. John Guare was the key witness against him and looked anything but comfortable on the stand.

David **H**ampton

He came to Gotham from cold Buffalo

    And sought to make his mark upon the stage,

But found his progress was extremely slow

    To place his name upon a Playbill page.

Accordingly, he tried to get ahead

    By acting out a fantasy he'd made

In order to obtain free board and bed

    From people who enjoyed the masquerade.

He posed as Sidney Poitier's heir and son,

    And when the truth was finally clear at last,

The dupes informed the playwright what he'd done

    So that a drama could be written fast.

They've made a million dollars from his story,

    But yet they want to keep both cash and glory.

Robert Alton Harris, who was put to death on April 21, 1992, was the first defendant to be executed in California's gas chamber since the Supreme Court resumed capital punishment in 1976. It was his claim that the use of cyanide gas was prohibited by the Eighth Amendment's stricture against "cruel and unusual punishment," a contention which some judges in that state believed deserved serious consideration by the Supreme Court. Accordingly, one of these jurists issued a stay of Harris' execution even while he was strapped to one of the two metal perforated chairs in the gas chamber at San Quentin Prison. However, the Supreme Court, working through the evening hours, set aside the stay and Harris was duly executed. Many years before, Barbara Graham (who, with a boyfriend, had been involved in a murder committed during a hold up) was informed by a guard as she entered the hermetically sealed execution chamber that she should just breathe heavily when the cyanide gas was released and she would feel no pain. "How do you know?" was her response.

The Execution of **R**obert **A**lton **H**arris

The State of California had rehearsed

    For months to have its guards avoid each glitch,

So that its cyanide would kill the first

    Condemned in many years without a hitch.

Despite a claim that gaseous homicide

    Had been prohibited as much too cruel,

The High Court overruled each judge who tried

    To give the victim time to prove this rule.

At three, they strapped him in the metal chair

    And started to prepare the acid bath,

When suddenly the telephone's shrill blare

    Snatched him for hours from the fatal path.

The Justices sat up all through the dark

    To ascertain that death would hit its mark.

Alcee Hastings, appointed to the federal bench in Florida by President Carter, was the first black in that state's history to attain that position. From the moment he was confirmed by the Senate, it was obvious that he was not going to be a run-of-the-mill jurist. He refused to be sworn in at the courthouse in Miami, as was the custom, but insisted on taking his oath of office on the stage of a predominantly black high school. He also rendered some of the first humanitarian decisions concerning the treatment of Haitian refugees in this country. When Ronald Reagan became President, Judge Hastings lost no time in publicly criticizing him as the representative of only the wealthy. Accordingly, it was not long before he was indicted for allegedly taking a bribe in a case involving organized crime defendants. At his trial, he represented himself and was acquitted. He was then impeached by the House of Representatives and convicted by the Senate on the same charges as had been made in the criminal case and was stripped of his judgeship. Along with other lawyers, I represented him in a lawsuit which contended that only a Senate committee of twelve, instead of the full Senate, had heard the evidence against him, which we contended was a violation of the explicit language of the Constitution. When a lower federal court agreed with us, the decision so impressed the voters of his Congressional District that he was elected to the House in 1992. Today, he is serving in that body with many of the same members who voted to impeach him four years earlier. As one civil rights leader once put it, "What goes around comes around."

The Lynching of **A**lcee **H**astings

This judge refused his swearing-in at court

    And held the ritual at an all-black school;

He brought the white establishment up short

    By dubbing Reagan as the rich man's tool.

He stated Haitian immigrants in jail

    Should not be treated as a lesser kind;

He said the legal system had to fail,

    So long as it was far from color-blind.

At first, they charged him with a venal crime,

    But when a jury found him free from guilt,

They had a shot at him a second time

    And now they drove the sword in to the hilt.

We scarce have need of any printed sign—

    A black upon the bench must toe the line.

On February 2, 1988, two armed Native Americans, Eddie Hatcher and Timothy Jacobs, entered the offices of the *Robersonian*, a newspaper published in Lumberston, N.C. They held the paper's employees hostage for nine hours until the Governor promised that he would investigate their charges that county officials were deeply involved in the drug trade. After they released their hostages, they were charged with violations of federal hostage taking and weapons statutes. After they were acquitted by a jury in Raleigh, N.C., they were then indicted under state kidnapping statutes. They eventually pled guilty, resulting in the early release of Jacobs. However, Hatcher, who was regarded as the ring leader, is still serving his sentence.

To Eddie Hatcher and Timothy Jacobs

They walked into the place, each with a gun,

    And promised that they meant no injury;

They did not point their arms at anyone

    And let the fearful and the sick go free.

Their purpose was to reach the Governor's ear

    So that official crime could be curtailed,

And Indians and blacks not live in fear

    Of a judicial system that had failed.

Throughout the history of this strife-torn land,

    There have been times when unheard words were said,

When tea was derricked by a Boston band

    And slavery ended with a million dead.

To treat these two like demons of the night

    Is to forget the wrongs they sought to right.

Tom Hayden was a charter member of the Chicago Eight and responsible for much of the articulation of the goals of Students for a Democratic Society (SDS) in the 1960s. When he was sentenced by Judge Julius Hoffman after being found guilty of a single minor charge, the judge stated that he believed that, of all the defendants in the case, Hayden had the best chance to make it in America. Hoffman was an accurate prophet because Tom returned to California where he first tried unsuccessfully to win the Democratic nomination for United States Senator. Nothing daunted, he then won seats in the state's Assembly and Senate. He startled his supporters in 1987 when he said that he favored the imposition of the death penalty in certain cases. I was so angered at what I considered outright pandering to the electorate that I wrote this sonnet, which appeared in several California newspapers, resulting in angry letters to me from both Hayden and his then wife, Jane Fonda.

"**H**ayden Criticized by Political Allies Over His Support of **D**eath **P**enalty"

LOS ANGELES TIMES HEADLINE

When Julius Hoffman sentenced Tom to jail,

    He said, with just a hint of inner glee,

Of all the culprits, you could never fail

    To make your way in our society.

So Tom went out to prove the old judge right,

    And, with the earnings of his actress wife,

He set a Senate seat within his sight

    And promised all a libertarian life.

But when he found that goal was much too high,

    He settled for a lesser piece of toast,

Content to wait a little while to try

    Another leap at a more tempting post.

In order to prepare for his next stride,

    He's opted for San Quentin's cyanide.

HINTS &
ALLEGATIONS

91

On the evening of November 3, 1990, a number of police officers responded to a report of a family fight in the apartment of Mary Mitchell in the Melrose section of the Bronx. When they arrived there, Officer Arno Herwerth shot and killed the 41-year-old Mitchell from a distance of four feet away. Although he admitted that the victim was bleeding from her head before he fired at her, Herwerth claimed that he had not hit her with his nightstick. Instead, he said that the 5'2" woman had seized the nightstick from him and attacked him with it. Upon the advice of his attorney, the officer refused to give a statement to his superiors and was eventually charged with first degree manslaughter. He elected to be tried by a judge alone and, on October 19, 1991, was acquitted.

The Indictment of
Police Officer **A**rno **H**erwerth

The policeman shot and took the woman's life

    Because, he said, he feared she'd kill him first,

Despite the fact she had no gun or knife,

    And proved that New York's "Finest" had its worst.

The killer stood three feet or so away

    And point-blank fired at his victim's heart,

Convinced that he would never have to pay

    For acting out the white man's lynching part.

Instead of murder, he's charged with less

    And freed without the posting of a bail;

His innocence his fellow cops profess

    Who know the normal system will prevail.

For, in the end, the jury will be waived

    So that this man can by a judge be saved.

After President Bush named Clarence Thomas to succeed to Thurgood Marshall's seat on the Supreme Court, Anita Hill, a law professor at the University of Oklahoma, came forward and informed the Senate Judiciary Committee that the nominee had sexually harassed her when they both worked at the Equal Employment Opportunity Commission (EEOC) many years earlier. Her charges resulted in televised hearings before the Committee which then was composed of only white men. Many of its members, while denying that they possessed any sexist attitudes, proceeded to interrogate Hill in a manner that belied their pious disclaimers. Two in particular, Pennsylvania's Arlen Specter and Orin Hatch of Idaho, lost no opportunity, no matter how tenuous, to attempt to sully Prof. Hill. Although the Committee split evenly on whether to recommend that the full Senate confirm Thomas, it was referred by Chairman Joseph Biden to the floor, and the nominee was seated by a vote of 52 to 48, the narrowest margin in history.

The Ordeal of **A**nita **H**ill

Each of the Senators was white and male

    And had no realistic sense of why,

When she was treated like an easy quail,

    The woman had not shouted to the sky.

The President soon let his cohorts see

    That the accuser should be made to look

As if her charges were pure fantasy

    Or she longed for a movie or a book.

The members of the panel missed no chance

    To swear that they had struggled every day

In an attempt to end each leering glance

    And sexist word that plagued each woman's way.

But when they started to interrogate,

    They quickly relapsed to their sexist state.

Late in the evening of December 20, 1986, a crowd of a dozen infuriated Italian-Americans beat and chased three blacks who had entered a pizzeria in Howard Beach, a virtually all-white enclave in Queens, N.Y., to call for help after their car broke down in the vicinity. When they ran in panic from their attackers, one, 23-year-old Michael Griffith, was killed by a car while crossing a major highway. At the same time, his uncle, Cedric Sandiford, was overtaken by the mob and severely beaten with a baseball bat. Three of the attackers were later convicted of manslaughter, assault, and conspiracy, and sentenced to maximum prison terms of fifteen, nineteen, and thirty years, respectively. Three others, who were convicted of 2nd degree riot, were given sentences of probation and community service, but no jail time, provided they agreed not to appeal their convictions.

The **H**oward **B**each Verdicts

The city waited breathlessly to hear

    What penalties the jury would impose

Upon the thugs who, in the night last year,

    Gave Michael Griffith's life an early close.

One day beyond the anniversary

    Of sudden death so long before its time,

The panel said that, of the six, just three

    Were guilty only of a lesser crime.

To some, the judgments were a welcome prize,

    The vindication of the rule of law;

To others, they were just a compromise

    That served to hide the system's fatal flaw.

But don't forget a black man had to die,

    So stay alert and keep your powder dry.

During the 1992 Presidential Campaign, Bill Clinton, in a speech to the Rainbow Coalition in Chicago, blasted Sister Souljah, a black rap artist, who had written songs that supported the so-called rioters in South Central Los Angeles after the return of the verdicts acquitting all the police officers charged with beating Rodney King. Not to be outdone, Vice-President Dan Quayle ripped into Ice-T, another black rap performer, for creating lyrics criticizing police officers. It all goes to show that both Republican and Democratic Parties will pander to white voters whenever it serves their purposes.

Hypocrisy, **A**merican Style

When Sister Souljah spoke in irony,

    Reacting to rebellion in L.A.,

The Democrat sensed opportunity

    And shocked the Rainbow with a bitter "Nay!"

Then, Mr. Quayle, not to be left behind,

    Claimed Ice-T was one of the nation's blights

For rapping cops were something less than kind

    When they had Third World suspects in their sights.

The honkies urge the blacks to sing their songs

    Like "We Shall Overcome" and all the rest,

And recommend that everyone belongs

    To groups that say nonviolence is the best.

The words of rage are never nice to hear,

    But white America must lend an ear.

When Dr. King made his unforgettable speech during the 1963 civil rights March on Washington, he thrilled his listeners to their core when he said that "I have a dream" that racial equality might soon become a reality in the United States. Thirty years later, within the space of a few short months, a helpless Rodney King was savagely beaten by a bevy of white Los Angeles police officers, a black man was set on fire in Florida by two white ones, a black undercover agent was gunned down by his white colleagues during a buy and bust drug operation in New York City, and a Detroit ghetto was besieged by enraged whites. In addition, young black males were being warehoused in penitentiaries across the nation and their brutalizers hastily exonerated by race-oriented criminal justice systems. It is tragically apparent that Dr. King's dream, no matter how hopefully expressed, is still light years away from realization.

"I Have a Dream"

"I have a dream," he said, in Washington,

    Some thirty years ago, at summer's grace,

That all Americans would be as one

    Regardless of their color or their race.

Today they're torching blacks in Florida

    And shoot an undercover blood right here;

They beat them down in California

    And in Detroit create a reign of fear.

The judges and the juries all make sure

    That every brutalizer will go free;

The system sees to it that most stay poor

    And young men sacrifice their liberty.

The words were marvelous, dear Dr. King,

    But time has proved they didn't mean a thing.

In 1992, while people were starving to death in Somalia, being mangled by mortar and heavy artillery fire in Sarajevo, fighting for the return of former Arab land in what used to be called Palestine, dying from Israeli air strikes in southern Lebanon, and trying to survive unconscionable trade boycotts in both Cuba and Iraq, what dominated the news on these shores was the bitter courtroom battle between Mia Farrow and Woody Allen. The horrendous human tragedies taking place all over the world were virtually ignored as Americans were titillated by Allen's love affair with his adopted daughter, Soon-Yi, and Farrow's claims that he had sexually molested one of their young children. That such a preoccupation by the public with what was, after all, a private war between two affluent celebrities, could take precedence over events that affected hundreds and thousands of people in other countries was possibly the most compelling evidence of the mundane nature of our priorities.

The **I**mportant **T**hings in Life

They're dying in Somalia, but the press

    Is filled with Mia's charges of abuse;

In Bosnia, life is a game of chess,

    While here we pray that Woody calls a truce.

The Palestinians fight for their old land

    But Soon-Yi's love affair is always new;

In Cuba and Iraq imports are banned,

    Ignored by Life and Time and Newsweek, too.

The Lebanese exist from day to day,

    Much less important than the Allen claim;

The inner city blight has gone away,

    Swept off the news by Farrow's cries of "Shame."

With so much stress on things of no-account,

    There's hardly space for those that really count.

In August of 1989, two blacks were shot to death, one in California and the other in Brooklyn. On Tuesday, August 22nd, 47-year-old Huey K. Newton, a co-founder of the Black Panther Party for Self-Defense, was gunned down at dawn in a drug-infested area of West Oakland. Shot three times in the head, he was pronounced dead at Highland Hospital at 6:12 a.m. Ojo Peda, a Nigerian exchange student, scooped up some of Newton's blood in a coffee cop, stating to passersby, "That blood is highly symbolic." Newton's assailant, 25-year-old Tyrone Robinson, claimed that he had shot in self-defense, but was eventually convicted of murder and sentenced to 32 years in prison. The day after Newton's death, 16-year-old Yusef K. Hawkins was attacked by a gang of thirty white youths in the Bensonhurst section of Brooklyn who, while shouting racial epithets, beat him to the ground with a baseball bat. 19-year-old Joseph Fama, urged on by Keith Mondello, then killed him with one shot from a handgun. On June 11, 1990, after a tumultuous trial, Fama was sentenced to a term of 32 2/3 to life, following his conviction of 2nd degree murder, while Mondello, described by his judge as the "catalyst" of the murder, was found guilty of riot, menacing, and false imprisonment, and received 5 1/3 to 16 years.

In **M**emoriam I:

YUSEF K. HAWKINS AND HUEY P. NEWTON

The two were shot 3000 miles apart,

    United only by their common race;

The one had given self-defense a start,

    The other was too young to know his face.

In death, they symbolize the genocide

    That seems to be the order of the day

And daily swells the list of those who've died

    Because they chose to walk a freer way.

How many solemn funerals must there be

    Before the senseless killings finally cease,

And when will Whitey ever start to see

    That without justice there can be no peace?

Now is the time to make the message plain—

    There is no bullet that's a one-way lane.

It is one of the most sinister of hypocrisies that, the moment political dissidents are dead, a street, a school, a park, or a public housing project is named after them. In New York, for example, we have a Martin Luther King, Jr. High School, a Malcolm X Boulevard, and an Albizu Campos Plaza Housing Project. Dr. King was shot to death after it was made clear by the FBI that he was a threat to his country, thus inspiring a susceptible James Earl Ray to murder. The enmity between Malcolm X and Elijah Muhammad was exacerbated by the Bureau through the use of fabricated anonymous letters and other dirty tricks designed to incite violence, eventually resulting in the former's assassination in 1965. Don Pedro Albizu Campos, the leader of the Puerto Rican independence movement, was jailed for years in a federal prison, a sentence that wrecked his health and brought on his premature death. Once each man was safely out of the way, his name was duly memorialized.

Albizu Campos waged a lifelong fight

    For independence of his native land;

The government, afraid that win he might,

    Destroyed him on a stateside prison strand.

For Malcolm X, the road was hard indeed,

    As Mr. Charlie hated what he said;

When bombs and poisoned food did not succeed,

    They used their firearms to shoot him dead.

The FBI did everything it could

    So Dr. King would raise a looney's fear;

By promulgating lies, it understood

    That someone soon would get the message clear.

Now that these three are safely in the ground,

    Their names on streets and parks and schools abound.

Late in the afternoon of August 19, 1991, in Brooklyn, N.Y., a car driven by Yosef Lifsh, a Hassidic Jew, jumped the curb and crashed into two young black children, 7-year-old Gavin Cato and his cousin, Angela, badly injuring the girl and killing Gavin. After the driver ran from the scene, a crowd of black residents quickly assembled, inaugurating three days of what has been referred to as the Crown Heights riots, during which Yankel Rosenbaum, a 29-year-old Australian ultra-orthodox Jew, was stabbed to death. Lifsh soon left for Israel and the efforts of black leaders to bring him back to the United States to answer for young Cato's death all failed. Lemrick Nelson, Jr., a 17-year-old black youth, was eventually tried for Rosenbaum's slaying but was acquitted by a jury of the crime. He is scheduled to be tried once more, this time in federal court, for his alleged violation of Rosenbaum's civil rights.

In Memory of All the **G**avin **C**atos

A young boy died upon a Brooklyn street,

 Who never lived beyond his seven years,

And spawned another wave of marching feet

 To symbolize a grief too deep for tears.

Now, Gavin Cato joins the ghostly band

 Of Clifford, Michael, Randy, and the rest,

Each one a grossly murdered young black male,

 Cut down by car or gun or throat compressed.

Why is it hard to understand the rage,

 Unleashed by each new onslaught on our youth,

When bigotry takes always center stage

 As people struggle to obtain the truth?

It does no good to try to slake the thirst

 Of those who cry that justice must come first.

On May 4, 1970, the Ohio National Guard shot four students, two women and two men, to death, and wounded nineteen others, on the campus of Kent State University, forty miles west of Cleveland. The shootings triggered the closing of some 300 American colleges and universities, causing President Nixon to end the American incursion into Cambodia, the event that had generated the anti-war demonstrations at Kent State leading to the May 4th tragedy. Immediately after the shootings, I was asked to come to the university but was not permitted to enter the campus. The students finally made alternative arrangements with the owner of the Kove, a student hangout in town, where I addressed a wall-to-wall crowd. I promised to form a legal team if any students or faculty members were indicted over the May 4th protests. When such charges were finally leveled, I arranged with Ramsey Clark and a number of progressive attorneys to stand up for the defendants. The result was that, after considerable legal maneuvering, few defendants were tried, and no one went to jail. As often as I can, I return to Kent State on the anniversary of the shootings, both out of respect for those who died or were wounded there and to keep the memory of an awful moment in American history painfully alive.

Kent **S**tate Revisited

Can it be true that it's been eighteen years

    Since Blanket Hill soaked up the youthful blood

Of those whose only crimes were earnest tears

    For each who died in Southeast Asian mud?

They are united now, who fell upon this hill,

    With all who dropped 10,000 miles away,

Destroyed by those they came so far to kill,

    They never lived beyond the Fourth of May.

Today, they perish still around the world,

    Their veins have not forgotten how to bleed;

The flags of lunacy remain unfurled

    And earth does not yet comprehend the need.

So now, as then, impatiently we yearn

    To know at last, "When will they ever learn?"

In November of 1961, in Nashville, Tennessee, I met Dr. King for the first time in a motel dining room. I must admit that, despite the enormous publicity that surrounded him, I did not know what he looked like in person. I was amazed to see that he was ten years younger than me and did not in the slightest resemble the Old Testament saint I had envisioned. When he asked me whether I would consider becoming what he called his special trial counsel, I asked for time to think it over. Later that night, I heard him speak for the first time and I was so enthralled by the tone and quality of his voice that I couldn't wait to tell him that I accepted his offer. Until his murder in Memphis seven years later, I gladly responded to every call from him, summonses that led me to such places as Birmingham, Montgomery, and Selma, Alabama, Atlanta and Albany, Georgia, Danville and Richmond, Virginia, Edenton, North Carolina, St. Augustine, Florida, and Jackson, Mississippi, among others. His assassination on April 4, 1968, when he was gunned down by a single bullet to the neck on the balcony of the Lorraine Motor Inn, now a civil rights museum, brought to a sudden and tragic end his pilgrimage for equal civil rights and liberties for all Americans, regardless of the color of their skins.

Martin Luther King, Jr.

Before we met, I thought that he would be

    A dark-skinned replica of Old John Brown,

A partisan of righteous fantasy,

    A would-be martyr waiting for his crown.

When we were introduced, so long ago,

    I could not bring myself to understand

This smallish man with close-cropped hair would know

    The special route to reach the Promised Land.

That night I heard him preach to all who came

    To hear the prophet of a new refrain,

And I knew then as well as my own name

    That I would never be myself again.

There is no dream that dies as hard as one

    That seemed so very close to being won.

When a small army of white Los Angeles police officers brutally attacked a supine black man with batons and kicks, they did not realize that a civilian was busy videotaping them from a building across the street. The airing of those tapes caused a wave of revulsion across the nation, forcing the Los Angeles District Attorney to obtain the indictments of four of the officers involved. However, the cases were transferred for trial in Simi Valley, a suburban community northwest of Los Angeles with few black residents. There, an all-white jury, even after viewing the videotapes of the assaults on King, acquitted each defendant. The result was a massive uprising in South Central Los Angeles during which fifty-two people were killed and an untold number of buildings burned to the ground. The ferocity of the reaction to the Simi Valley verdicts led the federal authorities to indict the four defendants on civil rights violations. After a trial in Los Angeles, two were convicted and two acquitted, an obvious compromise by a jury that didn't want to see a repetition of what the white press referred to as "riots," but did not want to overmuch infuriate the police.

The Acquittals of
Rodney **K**ing's Assailants

They beat the helpless victim on the ground

    With many blows from flailing riot sticks,

Convinced no one but police would hear the sound

    Of agony increased by fists and kicks.

The officers involved in such brutality

    Were unaware a camera taped their mob,

These noble whites of the LAPD

    Who knew that this was just part of the job.

Then to make sure that they would never do

    A day in jail and get what they deserve,

Their trial was moved to where the blacks were few

    And none would ever on their jury serve.

A prophet once announced, at some time past,

    The chickens will come home to roost at last.

In 1986, a bomb exploded at the LaBelle night club in Berlin, killing an American serviceman. Because he falsely assumed that Libya had been responsible for the blast, President Reagan ordered a night air raid on Tripoli.

As a result, Col. Qaddafi's youngest child, a daughter, was killed, as were a number of civilians, and many buildings were destroyed. It was later determined that Syria, not Libya, was probably responsible for the LaBelle bombing. However, no apologies were offered by the Reagan Administration for its tragic error.

The **L**ibyan **S**trike

The President announced to all the land

    That Libya had lacked humanity,

And thirty bombers under his command

    Had dropped their deadly loads on Tripoli.

The triumph was complete, we later learned,

    Civilians and the leader's child destroyed,

An embassy and some apartments burned

    And where a naval high school stood, a void.

The press, without a single adverse word,

    Accepted fully what our madman swore,

And from the opposition nothing heard.

    Except in praise of lunacy galore.

But it was clear when all was done and said,

    The object was to strike Qaddafi dead.

Ben Linder was a young American engineer who went to Nicaragua to assist in efforts to furnish electricity to impoverished rural areas. His project, the building of dam, became a Contra target and he and two of his co-workers were shot to death at point blank range. This atrocity helped to spur the end of American military support for the Contras. He is buried, at his family's request, in Nicaragua.

To **B**en **L**inder

He went to Nicaragua with hope

    That he was one American who came

To help the country people learn to cope

    And not to denigrate or kill or maim.

He worked to make the healing current flow

    For those whose homes were always dark at night,

So eyes could see and thirsting minds could grow

    And terror flee the bringing of the light.

The Contras crept in silence through the trees,

    With weapons cocked and murder on their minds,

Until they shot their quarry to his knees

    And opened deadly fire from behind.

The bullets that destroyed his youthful day

    Were brought with dollars from the U.S.A.

Sergeant Clayton F. Lonetree, the son of a Navaho mother and a Winnebago father, followed a family tradition of military service and enlisted in the Marine Corps out of high school. He was eventually assigned to guard duty at the American Embassy in Moscow where he fell in love with a young Soviet woman on the Embassy staff. Her uncle, a KGB agent, persuaded him to turn over to him the Embassy's floor plans and telephone directory. When he was transferred to Vienna, his conscience bothered him and he revealed to a CIA officer known as "Little John" what he had done. At his courtmartial, where he was represented by Las Vegas attorney Michael Stuhff and myself, the military judge, a Navy captain, permitted a key CIA official to testify under an assumed name and drastically curtailed cross-examination of this individual and many other prosecution witnesses. Accordingly, Lonetree was convicted of espionage and sentenced to thirty (later reduced to twenty-five and then fifteen) years which he is presently serving at Fort Leavenworth, Kansas. Initially, the Marine Corps, prodded by President Reagan, sought to obtain the death penalty by falsely charging that Lonetree had permitted Russian agents to invade the top secret code room. When the young black Marine who was expected to testify to this allegation insisted that it was untrue, it was quickly dropped. Today, we know from the debriefing of Aldrich Ames, the longtime CIA spy for the Russians, that Lonetree's case was created by the KGB to hide Ames' treachery. Now joined by Lonetree's military prosecutor, Stuhff and I are trying again to free him.

The Ordeal of Sergeant Lonetree

The sergeant stationed at the Moscow post

    Had disobeyed the order of the Corps

And fraternized with women of the host

    To fill the silence of a foreign shore.

The State Department, panicked by this news,

    Decided that the time was ripe to free

Itself of guilt by trumpeting its views

    The sergeant tried to aid the KGB.

The government strove to make this so

    By fabricating facts to meet the need

And utilizing strategy to sow

    Each fully false incriminating seed.

They thought that they could hang the sergeant high

    And thus the cup of blame would pass them by.

Alton Maddox, a Georgia native, left his home state in order to practice in New York City. Although his aggressive style enabled him to win a number of highly controversial criminal cases, it did not endear him to the legal establishment. After he became one of the attorneys for Tawana Brawley, an upstate black teenager who claimed that she had been raped by a sextet of white men, then Attorney General Robert Abrams filed a grievance against him with a disciplinary committee which was based on his conduct in that case. He was suspended from practice three years ago, while he was in the middle of a trial, and has not practiced since. After a lengthy hearing, at which I and many other witnesses testified on his behalf, he was suspended on August 1, 1994, for another five years which is tantamount to disbarment. He is the second progressive black lawyer in New York City to be suspended within two months, and a third, C. Vernon Mason, also active in the Brawley case, is in grave danger of meeting with the same fate.

The Suspension of **A**lton **M**addox

The state's Attorney General couldn't wait

    To file his grievances against a pair

Of black attorneys who had dared to rate

    His handling of Tawana's case unfair.

For Alton, born among the Georgia pine,

    New York had seemed a racial paradise,

Until he found the Mason-Dixon Line

    Did nothing to drown out the bigot's cries.

He fought the white establishment each day

    And so brought down its unforgiving ire;

It labored hard to find an easy way

    To rid the bar of all his righteous fire.

It wouldn't even pause a decent while,

    Suspending in the middle of a trial.

Each year, on May 19th, the birthday of Malcolm X, I write another sonnet to commemorate the day. While I never represented him, we were friends. I regarded him as a most unique man and am convinced that the FBI, in its infamous COINTELPRO program, designed to prevent the rise of what J. Edgar Hoover referred to as a "Black Messiah," created the climate which resulted in Malcolm's assassination on February 21, 1965, moments before he was to address a roomful of his followers in Manhattan's Audubon Ballroom.

Malcolm's Sixty-Seventh Birthday

MAY 19, 1992

He lives today as if he never died,

    Who shares his natal day with Ho Chi Minh,

And in his stint on earth so strongly tried

    To teach the whites the nature of their sin.

He would have pointed out that in L.A.,

    A revolution not a riot raged,

And that there'll never be a better day

    Until intolerance is finally caged.

This is the time to think of what he said

    And how he set an angry moral tone;

His words are loud, his lips are far from dead,

    He tells us all that we are not alone.

Across the land, we understand the X

    May in the future salvage all our necks.

When Spike Lee asked me to play the role of the racist Massachusetts judge who sentenced Malcolm X to eight to ten years in that state's penitentiary, I had mixed feelings. I had a long personal relationship with Malcolm, beginning with his appearance on March 3, 1960, on "Pro and Con," a program I conducted weekly on WMCA, a New York radio station. When the scene was filmed, I had a strong urge to give Denzel Washington, who played the title role and bore an uncanny resemblance to Malcolm, a suspended sentence, but Spike warned me that, if I did that, I would be replaced by an actor willing to follow the script. I have seen the film many times, and I still feel queasy about giving my old friend such a long sentence. However, as Supreme Court Justice Felix Frankfurter once remarked, history has its due.

"Malcolm X"—The Film

The film begins with Rodney King's ordeal

    And then this country's flag is wholly burned;

It ends with how the young black children feel

    About the man whose life they just have learned.

Between these points, there is the history

    Of one who conked his hair to seem near-white,

Who spent his early years in burglary,

    And the forbidden pleasures of the night.

But then, in jail, he heard the spirit's call

    And soon became the strident voice of hope,

Determined that the walls of hate would fall

    And that his words would cut each racist rope.

Today, he speaks to us far from the grave

    And says, "Stand up, be firm, be just, be brave."

On February 11, 1990, Nelson Mandela, accompanied by his wife, Winnie, walked out of Robben Island, where he had been imprisoned for some twenty-six years. A little more than four years later, he was elected President of the Republic of South Africa, after a campaign in which blacks were allowed, for the first time in that country's history, to participate as free and equal citizens.

The Liberation of **N**elson **M**andela

The prison gates at last creaked open wide

    To let the captive walk to freedom now,

With beaming Winnie marching by his side.

    And sunlight dancing on his wrinkled brow.

The hair was gray, the body old and frail,

    But every step was firmer than the last;

Like knights of Camelot who sought the Grail,

    He strode into the future from the past.

"Amandla!" he shouted to the crowd,

    His voice as strong as thirty years ago,

And then, his speech in hand, he stood up proud,

    Prepared once more to strike against the foe.

The world is changing everywhere, it seems,

    Now is the time for fleshing out his dreams.

When Thurgood Marshall announced his retirement in 1991, it gave George Bush a welcome opportunity to fill the seat of this liberal Justice with a nominee who would continue the process of wrecking the Bill of Rights. The President wasted no time in naming Clarence Thomas to the seat. This sonnet, written before Thomas' nomination, accurately prophesied that Marshall's replacement would be the judicial equivalent of Eugene "Bull" Connor, the Public Safety Commissioner of Birmingham, Alabama, during the civil rights struggles of the 1960s who used firehoses and attack dogs, among other things, to end Dr. King's anti-segregation marches in that city.

Exit **T**hurgood **M**arshall
—Enter **B**ull **C**onnor

With Thurgood Marshall finally off the court,

    The President is free to fill his seat

With one who'd sell the Constitution short

    And stampede civil rights to full retreat.

The new majority will do its best

    To speed up executions everywhere,

To lay Roe versus Wade to early rest,

    And wreck the Bill of Rights beyond repair.

The gains of yesteryear will soon be lost

    Unless a lot of people understand

The monumental impact of the cost

    Upon the forward progress of our land.

No southern sheriff has ever done much worse

    To put our liberties into a hearse.

In 1964, a thousand white students from all over the United States, under the leadership of the Council of Federated Organizations (COFO), converged on Mississippi with a mission to register to vote as many blacks as possible and set up Freedom Schools throughout the state. Shortly after their arrival, James Chaney, a local black youth, Michael Schwerner, a white Congress of Racial Equality (CORE) worker, and Andrew Goodman, a New York City college student, were accosted in Neshoba County and murdered by law enforcement officers. Their bodies were not found for almost a month, until a reward offered by the FBI of $25,000.00 succeeded in obtaining the information that they had been buried under a dam site. Eventually, some of their killers, including the Neshoba County Sheriff and one of his deputies, were tried in federal court for violating their civil rights and sentenced to relatively short prison terms. Despite the murders, only two of the students returned home and, before the summer was out, 60,000 blacks had been registered and many Freedom Schools had been established. Thirty years later, many of the original COFO volunteers, including my daughter Karin, returned to a far different Mississippi than the state they had left in 1964. This sonnet was included in the official program of the 1994 reunion.

Mississippi **S**ummer Revisited

It's hard to comprehend that thirty years

    Have come and gone since nineteen sixty-four

When northern students conquered all their fears

    And journeyed south to do their bit and more.

Despite the atmosphere of bitter hate,

    They helped some 60,000 blacks enroll,

And set up Freedom Schools throughout the state,

    Although quick violence took an awful toll.

The sheriff thought the volunteers would run

    By shooting down our Mickey, Andy and James,

But it took more than murders with a gun

    To make committed youths forget their aims.

Three decades from the past, they have returned

    To find peace where once Mississippi burned.

At dawn on Friday, October 18, 1985, Benjamin Moloise, a 30-year-old black poet and a strong supporter of the outlawed African National Congress, was hanged in Pretoria's Central Jail for the murder of a South African police officer three years earlier. President P.W. Botha, despite pleas from Pope John II, the United Nations Security Council, and a host of other international individuals and organizations, refused to halt the execution. The evening before, police fired tear gas into the home of Moloise's mother and later she was not permitted to see her son before he was hanged, but was permitted to look at his closed coffin after his death. "The government is cruel," she said, "It is really, really cruel." Severe clashes between whites and 3,000 enraged blacks took place in central Johannesburg after the news of Moloise's execution became known.

The Execution of **B**enjamin **M**oloise

Framed by its brilliant jacaranda trees,

    Pretoria's Central Jail, in dreary tones,

Awaits the end of poet Moloise

    With no more feeling than its ancient stones.

The gallows stands beneath the mammoth dome

    That caps the prison's execution hall

With its expectant noose, like roads to Rome,

    The central point from each encircling wall.

"This government is cruel," his mother said,

    In trying for a last look at her son,

But was not told that she could go inside

    Until the murder by the state was done.

They pleaded from all corners of the map;

    Still Botha let the hangman spring the trap.

For years, white police officers in the City of New York have gunned down or otherwise dispatched young black males. Their victims have ranged from nine-year-old Clifford Glover, shot in the back, to graffiti artist Michael Stewart who was strangled near Manhattan's Union Square. Even an honor student at the exclusive Phillips Exeter Academy, Edmund Perry, was shot dead in Central Park. Few of the officers involved were indicted by grand juries, and those who were charged opted for judge trials at which they were, with one exception, invariably acquitted. The exception, the officer who shot Clifford Glover, was found not guilty by reason of temporary insanity, and spent some time in a psychiatric facility before being returned to the community.

New York **D**eath **S**quads

It seems that every week we hear the news

    The cops have shot another black kid dead,

And then we're treated to official views

    The victims were the guilty ones instead.

The murderers are taken off the street

    Until grand juries wipe their records clear,

And then they're quickly put back on the beat,

    Prepared to kill whomever gets too near.

We have no need of lynch mobs anymore,

    The police provide a more efficient way

To better still perform this messy chore

    Without the worries of a judgment day.

We should recall that Malcolm did expound

    Whatever goes around must come around.

When Richard M. Nixon died on April 22, 1994, there was a frenzied outpouring of favorable hyperbole designed to make the public forget his tawdry past. Like millions of other Americans, I watched his funeral on television and could not believe the torrent of eulogies which emanated from the President of the United States and others. Could this possibly be the same man, I asked myself, who engineered the Watergate break-in, created the infamous "Enemies List," ordered the invasion of Cambodia which led to the murders of four students and the wounding of nineteen others on Kent State University's Blanket Hill, authorized the institution of "dirty tricks" against his political foes, sabotaged the democratic regime of Chilean President Salvador Allende, and hated blacks and Jews? It reminded me of a wag's quip many years ago that no one ever grew poor underestimating the intelligence of the American public.

The Death of **R**ichard M. **N**ixon

"HE CAME, HE SAW, HE CORRUPTED"

They dare to praise you now in tearful terms,

   The Kissingers, the Doles, and Clinton, too,

Forgetting how you fed our young to worms

   And made it hard to tell the false from true.

Your minions broke into the Watergate

   To tap the phones of your election foes;

You kept a list of those you learned to hate

   And added dirty tricks to all our woes.

You set the stage for death on Blanket Hill

   And brought the war in Asia home at last;

You tried to keep our protest voices still

   Until your bleak and ugly reign was past.

The blood, the lies, the hate—this trilogy

   Is now your only proper eulogy.

In 1977, Leonard Peltier, a member of the American Indian Movement (AIM), was convicted of the murders of two FBI agents who had been shot to death on South Dakota's Pine Ridge Indian Reservation on June 26, 1975. Peltier had been extradited from Canada on the basis of affidavits which the government now admits were fabricated. The key evidence against him at his trial in Fargo, N.D., was the testimony of an FBI firearms expert that a shell casing found near the agents' bodies had been ejected from a rifle falsely attributed to him. Many years after he had been sentenced to two successive life terms, it was revealed that a report by this same firearms expert, which had been hidden from the defense, stated that the shell casing could not possibly have been fired from the weapon in question. Despite this revelation, Peltier was unable to obtain reversals of his convictions and a new trial and the Supreme Court refused to review his case.

The government withheld the key report

    That proved Peltier was innocent;

No juror sitting in that Fargo court

    Was told about the hidden document.

The judge, who sided with the FBI

    And followed closely in its tracks,

Refused to let our Leonard further try

    To show another panel all the facts.

While conscious of the evidential flaw,

    The higher court denied a second trial;

In doing so, it overlooked the law

    And let its prejudice thus close the file.

We celebrate the Constitution's birth

    And praise our fairness all around the earth.

Sam, a cockapoo (half-cocker, half-poodle) was part of my family for almost all of his life. When he reached sixteen years or so, it was obvious that he was nearly at the end of the trail. Finally, it was time to say goodbye to him and let the veterinarian put him out of his obvious misery. Everyone who has ever put down a pet can understand the grief and anguish felt by the humans who shared its all too short existence. After Sam died, we kept his collar and leash as poignant reminders that our home had once been graced by a companion who wanted nothing more than the joy of being with us.

An **O**ld **D**og Dies

An old dog dies and what is left behind,

    Outside of memories of other days,

Old ears which did not hear and eyes gone blind

    And legs that staggered in familiar ways.

An old dog dies and much is left behind,

    The sweeter memories of other days,

A tail that unfurled proudly in the wind

    Or fluttered fiercely to the sounds of praise.

An old dog dies and more is left behind

    Than empty collars and forgotten days

Or leashes one could never seem to find

    And whitened hair that washed out from the grays.

An old dog dies and takes with him a part

    Of all who reveled in his trusting heart.

In 1987, when President Reagan named William H. Rehnquist as his choice for Chief Justice, I testified against the nominee. I knew that, in his home state of Arizona, he had been involved in scaring black voters away from the polls, and that he had a summer home in New England in an area where blacks and Jews were excluded. He had also been the architect, as a Deputy Attorney General, of Richard Nixon's infamous justification for engaging in wiretapping without first obtaining a warrant, the so-called "national security" exception to the Fourth Amendment's command. It was based on this premise that Nixon ordered the tapping, in late May of 1972, of the telephone of Larry O'Brien, the chairperson of the Democratic National Committee (DNC), in its Watergate headquarters. Late on the night of Friday, June 15, 1972, when Frank Willis, a black security guard, noticed that the front door to the DNC was mysteriously ajar, he entered the premises and arrested a group known as the Plumbers who were attempting to remove the bug from O'Brien's phone, an incident that later led to the President's resignation. It has always been my theory that Rehnquist, then an Associate Justice, leaked a Supreme Court decision obtained by my organization, the Center for Constitutional Rights, outlawing the so-called "national security" exception, which was due to be made public on Monday, June 18th, thus removing any legal excuse for the Watergate bug. Four days later, the 18-minute gap occurred in the tape maintained by Nixon's secretary, Rosemary Woods, which may well have contained information that would have revealed the possible Rehnquist leak. I brought these suspicious coincidences to the attention of the Senate Judiciary Committee during the Rehnquist confirmation hearing, but only Senator Kennedy seemed interested and the matter died

144   aborning.

William H. **R**ehnquist

He brought his home where whites could live apart,

 And later still where Jews may not reside;

He railed against the laws that gave a start

 To freedom that had been so long denied.

He urged a prompt return to outworn goals

 When separate status was the legal rule;

He frightened new-born voters at the polls

 And fought to keep the segregated school.

He told the President he had the right

 To wiretap without a warrant's stay;

He never missed a chance to dim the light

 Ignited in a more heroic day.

The thought that such a man could lead the Court

 Might well have made the Framers self-abort.

Feminist Gloria Steinem once wrote an OpEd piece for *The New York Times* in which she opined that the public attitude about various crimes, such as Bernhard Goetz's shooting of four black youths or the rape-beating of the woman who came to be known as the Central Park Jogger would be far different if the races of the participants were reversed. Her observations were validated by the acquittals of six white students at St. John's University who were charged with deliberately plying a black woman student with alcohol and then committing a variety of sex acts upon her. There is no doubt in my mind that, if the victim had been white and her attackers black, the outcome of the trial would have been diametrically different.

Reversals

Imagine if young Yusef had been white

    And all his wanton murderers were black,

The media would scream with all its might

    And call the suspects animals on crack.

Suppose that Bernhard Goetz had been a blood

    And those he shot as white as driven snow,

In court his name would surely have been mud

    And he'd still have some prison years to go.

Just think that if the jogger in the park

    Had been a sister running toward her nest

When struck down by Caucasians in the dark,

    There'd be no talk of wilding and the rest.

Reversals make it very plain to see,

    A lot depends upon identity.

In recent days, the religious right has captured the Republican Party in Virginia and, by so doing, secured the nomination of Ollie North as its candidate for the United States Senate. In other states, these fanatics are in the ascendancy in party politics and it is expected that their candidates will appear on many ballots around the country this fall. Even the fact that some of their most popular television evangelists have been shown to have been guilty of sexual misconduct or outright thievery, the faithful still rally to the banners of bigotry and ignorance so flamboyantly waved by their successors.

The **R**ighteous **R**ight

OR, PRAISE THE LORD AND PASS THE GRAVY

They rail at those they think are soft on Reds

  And see abortion as the Devil's trash,

While they leap fast into adulterous beds

  And pay their lovers with the faithful's cash.

The Contras are their favorite charity,

  They look on Jesus as their bosom friend,

Their homilies are rank hypocrisy,

  They search for worlds and money without end.

They use the television waves to reach

  The masses with their burning platitudes,

Convinced that they alone are fit to preach

  The Gospel to the yearning multitudes.

They've found there's lots of moolah to be made

  From those who are of Hell so much afraid.

Just across the water from New York's LaGuardia Airport lies Rikers Island, the detention center for defendants awaiting trial in the city's criminal courts. It is perennially overcrowded, offers its inmates, mainly black and Latino, almost no educational or other programs, and has been the scene of many pitched battles between the prisoners and their guards. After one such confrontation, in which a number of inmates were wounded, some seriously, the guards blockaded the only access bridge to the institution and prevented ambulances from taking the wounded men to area hospitals. Many of the young prisoners, who sometimes wait years for their trials, would rather plead guilty, even if innocent, in order to be assigned to one of the upstate state facilities where many of the programs so sadly lacking at Rikers are available. It is not difficult to imagine what thoughts go through the minds of the inmates as they watch the planes leaving regularly from across the bay.

The island's supercrowded with the sort

    Who can't afford to meet their judges' bail,

Who'll wait for weeks or months to go to court

    And maybe some day free themselves from jail.

LaGuardia's planes fly overhead each hour

    While inmates wish that they could be aboard

And leave this place of penitential power

    Where little but the grapes of wrath are stored.

The walls of many cells are stained with red

    Where guards used clubs to prove that they stand tall,

With knowledge that their faithful "union" head

    Would blame it all on blacks at City Hall.

It takes a lot of courage for a hack

    To beat a prisoner who can't fight back.

Throughout the 1980s, when refugees attempted to flee from both Guatemala and El Salvador in order to avoid the Death Squads organized by the right wing governments in those countries, they were aided in their flight by many Americans of good will. However, instead of recognizing that those who helped the escapees were doing humanity a great and needed service, the United States began to charge them with violating federal statutes. Later, other Americans who wanted to take medical supplies and food to Cuba in the face of a cruel embargo found that their government did everything possible to interdict such shipments. However, by dint of determined perseverance on the part of those involved, most of the material found its way to Havana.

Sanctuary

The refugees stream in from far and near,

    One step ahead of Death Squads in their land,

And seeking only life without the fear

    That is the hallmark of their native strand.

In Guatemala and El Salvador,

    They cross the rivers and turn each bend

And slip toward sanctuary's open door,

    In hopes the time of terror's at an end.

When finally they reach their promised place,

    They find that those who helped them emigrate

Have been indicted for their act of grace

    By a vindictive and unfeeling state.

The huddled masses yearning to breathe free

    Must now look elsewhere for their liberty.

HINTS &
ALLEGATIONS

153

Some sixty years ago, nine black teenage youths were arrested in Scottsboro, Alabama, and charged with the rapes of two women on top of a freight car containing crushed stone. Quickly dubbed the Scottsboro Boys by the news media, they were immediately tried without lawyers and, with one exception, sentenced to death. Their convictions were set aside by the United States Supreme Court on the ground that they had been denied effective counsel at their brief trials. Eventually, their cause was adopted by the Communist Party and, one by one, the Boys, now grown men, were released when it became obvious that the supposed victims had perjured themselves. In 1989, a young white woman was raped in New York's Central Park and viciously beaten within an inch of her life. A number of black and Latino youths were quickly rounded up by the police and accused of the crimes. On appeal, I represented one of them—15-year-old Yusef Salaam—who was browbeaten into an oral confession by a white detective while his mother, aunt, and an Assistant United States Attorney who served as his Big Brother, were not permitted to see him.

Although his conviction was upheld by the Court of Appeals, New York's highest tribunal, the dissenting judge was appalled at the idea that a juvenile could be treated this way. It was obvious to me that those judges who upheld Yusef's conviction, all whites, were motivated by sheer and unadulterated racism.

Scottsboro Revisited?

The jogger lay for hours in the park,

    The victim of a rape beyond the pale,

Her agony well hidden by the dark,

    Her lifeblood dripping on the budding trail.

The police then rushed to tell the eager press

    The teenaged boys had laughed at what they'd done,

A few had been persuaded to confess

    That someone else had been the criminal one.

The white community had little care

    For any process, due or otherwise,

And mingled racial hatred with each prayer,

    Content to listen to the headlined cries.

They may be guilty, time alone will tell,

    But long before their trial, they're damned to hell!

first met Pete Seeger on a night flight to Jackson, Mississippi, in 1962. I knew that he was on the plane when I noticed his guitar case, adorned with freedom slogans, strapped into the seat next to him. He told me that he was making his annual pilgrimage to the grave of Huddie "Leadbelly" Ledbetter, the legendary blues singer and composer of such songs as "Good Night, Irene," and "Rock Island Line," who had died in 1949 and was buried in Baton Rouge, Louisiana. I persuaded him to disembark at Jackson where my daughter Karin was a transfer student at Tougaloo Southern Christian College, a virtually all-black institution just outside of the city. When we landed, I preceded him off the plane and my daughter rushed forward to greet me. When she saw who was behind me, she swerved, shouting "Pete Seeger!" and ran to embrace him. He played and sang at the college until 5:00 a.m. when we rushed him back to the airport to catch an early morning flight to Baton Rouge. Since then, I have run into Pete and his wife, Toshi, on many occasions and they both have always made themselves available for any worthwhile cause. This sonnet was written for them when they were honored by WESPAC, an umbrella civil rights organization in Westchester County, N.Y.

To **P**ete and **T**oshi **S**eeger

MARCH 18, 1990

They're quite a pair, our Toshi and our Pete,

    And they most certainly deserve this day;

They never sought avoidance of the heat

    Or chose to take the coward's easy way.

With song and speech, they've gone about their quest

    To bring about a cleaner rainbow world

Where accidental birth is not the test

    And prejudice's banners stay unfurled.

They ask us all, "When will we ever learn"

    That war is not the answer to our prayer,

And tell us that our fellow humans yearn

    For equal laws and justice that is fair.

Whenever they have heard the trumpets call,

    These two have never failed to stand up tall.

There are two highly controversial professors at New York's City College, white Michael Levin and black Leonard Jeffries. Levin has proclaimed for years that blacks are inherently inferior to whites, while Jeffries, in a bitter speech in Albany, among other things, blamed Jews in the movie industry for the derogatory portrayal of blacks in many films. The latter's remarks were highly publicized with the Anti-Defamation League of B'nai B'rith demanding that he be removed from his post as Chairperson of the Department of Black Studies. The College authorities capitulated and removed Jeffries from his position, only to have a federal judge later order his reinstatement on First Amendment grounds. No punitive action was ever taken against Levin.

Selective Blame

A Michael Levin can parade his trash

    And there's no public censure of his views,

But let a Leonard Jeffries be so rash,

    His words are featured on the evening news.

When Dr. Jeffries made his famous speech

    About the cinematic industry,

The Jews demanded he no longer teach

    Within a city university.

Yet, Dr. Levin has proclaimed for years

    That black is quite inferior to white,

Without a spate of vocal Jewish fears

    That what he said was morally not right.

It is, of course, a more than crying shame

    To thus engage in such selective blame.

HINTS &
ALLEGATIONS

159

It's passing strange that Virginia's Republicans have selected Ollie North as their 1994 Senatorial candidate. In 1986, it was revealed that he played a principal role in Ronald Reagan's illegal scheme to furnish Iran with arms in exchange for the release of a number of hostages held by groups friendly to the Teheran government. The funds received from the Iranians were then to be used to help finance the Contras in Nicaragua in their efforts to overthrow the Sandinista regime. He was eventually indicted and convicted of aiding and abetting an endeavor to obstruct Congress, destroying, obliterating, or revising National Security Council documents, and accepting an illegal gratuity. But an appellate court, on July 20, 1990, reversed his convictions on the ground that, when he took the Fifth Amendment in his appearance before Congress, he had been given immunity for his testimony.

Semper **F**idelis

He knew that Congress had a stringent rule

    That Uncle's cash could not facilitate

The Contra's ever urgent need to fuel

    Their war against the Sandinista state.

He found a way to circumvent the ban

    And sold the Ayatollah guns and tanks,

Depositing the profits from the plan

    In Switzerland's convenient secret banks.

When asked to tell the Congress what he did,

    He saw to it that he would not be blamed—

He raised his hand and took the oath, then hid

    Behind the Constitution he had shamed.

Are young Marines now urged to sally forth

    And serve their country like Light Colonel North?

Until very recently, the Senate Judiciary Committee, which passes on all federal judicial appointments as well as nominees for high-ranking positions in the Department of Justice, was composed only of white males. Although its function is to explore thoroughly the backgrounds of such individuals, it has usually served as a rubber stamp for whatever President occupied the White House. However, because of the high visibility of a number of Supreme Court nominees, such as Robert Bork and Clarence Thomas, during the past decade, its televised hearings have attracted significant national attention. When Anita Hill charged that Justice Thomas had been guilty of improper sexual advances toward her when they both worked at the Equal Employment Opportunity Commission (EEOC), the Committee's public hearings became more popular than television's soap operas. The electorate was treated to the spectacle of a synod of sexist white men who sought to support the nominee by degrading Hill in every way possible. One Senator accused her of lifting one of her examples of sexual harassment from the book, *The Exorcist*, while another implied that she was motivated solely because she had been spurned by Thomas. At the conclusion of the hearings, the Committee split evenly but voted to refer the nomination to the Senate floor. Thomas was ultimately confirmed by a vote of 52 to 48, the narrowest margin ever received by a successful Supreme Court nominee. Today, one can still see many people sporting buttons which read, "I believe Anita Hill," and Thomas has proved to be far to the right of Genghis Khan.

The **S**enate **J**udiciary **C**ommittee

Joe Biden grinned, the gavel in his hand,

    And saw that all obtained their time to shine,

While Thurmond used his accent to demand

    That this once-Georgia black complete the Nine.

Then Hatch relied upon "The Exorcist"

    As DeConcini played a neutral role,

And Simpson pointed to a hidden list

    To prove that Hill was never pure of soul.

Our Teddy was a prisoner of his past

    And Specter took the prosecutor's road,

While Metzenbaum was far too mild to blast

    His colleagues for the shameful row they'd hoed.

Each of the rest sat on his trousered male behind

    And swore that women's rights were always on his mind.

Thomas B. Galligan, a notoriously prosecution-oriented jurist, was the judge selected to try the so-called Central Park Jogger trials. The method by which particular judges are selected to preside over particular trials in New York is a mysterious one, but it is widely assumed that prosecutors play a major role in seeing to it that the choices are to their liking. For example, in the third trial of two ex-Black Panthers accused of killing a white police officer in 1980, the judge selected was the brother of a policeman and admitted that he numbered hundreds of officers among his acquaintances. Needless to say, the defendants, whose two prior trials before other judges had resulted in hung juries, were finally convicted. Although I was not his trial lawyer, I did represent Yusef Salaam at his sentencing on September 9, 1991. I sensed that Justice Galligan could hardly wait for the defendant and myself to finish our remarks before imposing the maximum sentence allowed by law.

Sentencing **D**ay at the Jogger Trial

The judge had waited long and patiently

    To do what he internally had vowed

By seeing to it that the hated three

    Received the maximum the law allowed.

In former days, the lynch mob used a rope

    And cheered as lifeless bodies danced on air;

Today, the court serves to extinguish hope

    With nothing for the sensitive to bear.

The black-robed man, with little in his head

    Except the joy of sending them to jail,

Heard not a thing they and their counsel said,

    Lost in the lure of his Unholy Grail.

He simmered while the lawyers had the floor,

    Then read the words he'd written long before.

Following their convictions by a federal jury of violating the civil rights of Rodney King, Los Angeles Police Officers Koon and Powell were given extremely light sentences of thirty months in jail by the white judge who presided over their trial. In sentencing them, he partially excused their conduct in beating their helpless victim while he lay prostrate on the ground by maintaining that King had been guilty of provoking his attackers. Luckily for Los Angeles, the judge's wholly unjustified remarks did not lead to the type of uprising that was generated by the acquittals rendered by a suburban jury a year earlier. Recently, an appellate court ruled that the sentences he imposed were much too light, and ordered a re-sentencing.

The Sentences of
Sergeant **K**oon and **O**fficer **P**owell

They'd been convicted of brutality

    And should have served at least six years in jail

For acts recorded for us all to see,

    A scene that went so far beyond the pale.

The judge put almost all the blame instead

    Upon the black man beaten on the ground;

The officers had been provoked, he said,

    Negating what the federal jury found.

He proved once more that, in Caucasian eyes,

    The Rodney Kings are valued like Dred Scott,

And that a minor term was no surprise

    From one who thinks that they're not worth a lot.

But if the cops were black, the victim white,

    The sentences would never be so light.

Two years ago, the New York Judicial Commission on Minorities, established by Governor Mario Cuomo and then Chief Judge Sol Wachtler, conducted an extensive investigation into the state's criminal justice system. In its final report, it concluded that there were two different systems of justice in New York, one for the whites, and one for everybody else. As an attorney who has practiced for almost a half-century in the criminal courts, both on the state and federal levels, I can verify that defendants whose skins are black get vastly different treatment than whites charged with the same crimes. Until this disparity disappears, the slogan, "No Justice, No Peace," will continue to resound in the ghettos of New York and every other urban center across the land.

The **S**kin **G**ame

A white who's charged with rape has naught to fear—

    The jury soon will put him in the clear.

A black indicted for that very crime

    Will surely get it in the neck each time.

A white who steals a fortune more or less

    Will get a year or two for his success.

A black who's found to rob a buck or two

    Must settle for a long term prison view.

A white who gives a black eternity

    Knows that at trial he'll usually go free.

A black who kills a white with gun or knife

    Will get the chair or go away for life.

The punishment is different for each sin,

    Depending on the color of your skin.

For years, deserted buildings on New York's Lower East Side have been occupied by homeless people with no other place in which to live. However, the police, urged by a number of Mayors, past and present, have made it a habit to evict them forcibly. This was the case for those who eked out a modicum of privacy in 319 East 8th Street, a condemned Manhattan tenement, in 1989, and who were dislodged, upon orders of then Mayor Edward I. Koch, by an army of officers. When the city attempted to raze the building so that it could make a profit out of a sale of a vacant lot, Bruce McM. Wright, a courageous black judge, directed that the wreckers cease their activity. However, the Mayor found a more tractable jurist who promptly overturned Wright's order and the building was then destroyed.

How to **H**andle **S**quatters

DEDICATED TO THE FORMER RESIDENTS OF 319 EAST 8TH STREET

The edifice was home to twenty-three

    Who otherwise would be without a cot;

The city wanted to be wholly free

    To make a profit with a vacant lot.

One gutsy judge attempted to prevent

    This perverse urban madness of the mind,

But Führer Koch found one to circumvent

    This order hours after it was signed.

And yet it took storm troopers by the score

    To keep the eager wreckers safe and sound

So they could rip each window and each door

    Until they razed the building to the ground.

The way, they say, to solve the homeless plight

    Must be to make some twenty more each night.

On March 1, 1990, six white male students at New York's St. John's University lured a Jamaican-born coed to one of their off-campus residences. There, she was plied with vodka in orange juice and then sodomized and otherwise mistreated. Felony charges were brought against the six, and the first trial in the summer of 1991, which lasted two-and-a-half months, resulted in the acquittals of three of the defendants. The acquittals generated cries of outrage from the black community. Two other defendants then pled guilty to reduced misdemeanor charges and were sentenced to a three-year term of probation. The victim then decided to press no further charges, stating that she wanted to get on with her life.

The **S**t. **J**ohn's Acquittals

If she were white and they had all been black,

 The jury never would have let them go,

And there would not have been a media lack

 Of headlines calling them the country's foe.

It hinges on the color of the skin

 Of victims and the ones accused of crime

To show just who will lose and who will win

 And which defendant gets some prison time.

It didn't matter what the jurors heard

 Of if the victim was in fact abused;

They never thought to doubt the white man's word,

 No matter how the woman had been used.

St. John's now knows that blacks who're sodomized

 Won't see their white assaulters criminalized.

In 1993, members of the Irish Lesbian and Gay Organization (ILGO) attempted to march under their own banner in the annual St. Patrick's Day Parade up New York's Fifth Avenue. The Ancient Order of Hibernians, which sponsored the march, refused to let them do so, a position that was sustained by Judge Kevin T. Duffy, a federal judge, who held that the parade was a "religious" rather than a "civic" event, even though, a year earlier, the Ancient Order had taken a diametrically different position. My partner, Ronald L. Kuby, and I then went into a New York State court and tried to obtain an order permitting ILGO to march. The parade's sponsor succeeded in transferring the case to Judge Duffy who refused to change his ruling. My daughters, Sarah and Emily, were arrested on the day of the parade when they joined other protesters in trying to obstruct the marchers.

St. **P**atrick's Day **P**arade

MARCH 17, 1993

The Ancient Order of Hibernians

    Was fearful that its march on Paddy's Day

Would be disgraced by gays and lesbians

    Who did not interact the "normal" way.

The patron saint, it claimed, would be aghast

    To see the ILGO banner held on high;

As for the cardinal, his ire was vast,

    His voice as strident as Bounty's Bligh.

"They shall not pass St. Patrick's door," he said,

    "Unless they walk without a flag or sign

Proclaiming what they do or don't in bed,

    So that there is no shaming of the shrine."

Yet, far above, the Lord of sun and shade

    Saw to it that it rained on their Parade.

In 1966, Morton Stavis, Arthur Kinoy, Benjamin Smith, and I formed the Center for Constitutional Rights, a legal and educational foundation which is still going strong. In addition to becoming the Center's vigorous President, Morty represented me in every one of my legal scrapes. He succeeded in getting an appellate court to reverse my contempt convictions growing out of the Chicago Conspiracy Trial which had resulted in the imposition of a prison sentence of four years and thirteen days. He managed to reduce a fine levied against two civil rights lawyers and myself by a North Carolina federal court for daring to institute a civil rights action against the Governor of that state and other officials from $122,000.00 to $43,000.00. He appeared for me in a New York disciplinary hearing growing out of my observation that the judge in the celebrated Central Park Jogger trial was unworthy of wearing the robe. These were just three of the matters in which he managed to keep me functioning as a lawyer for more than three decades. When he died suddenly, from a fall while visiting relatives in California, I initially felt resentment, then intense grief, that my longtime protector was no longer around. At the time of his death in December of 1992, he was scheduled to argue the appeal of Margaret Kelly Michaels, a young woman who had been sentenced to almost fifty years in a New Jersey prison for allegedly sexually abusing three- and four-year-old children at a day care center. Morty's widow and sons asked me to argue the case before a three-judge appellate court, which I did on February 1, 1993. Ms. Michael's conviction was reversed on the ground that she had received a terribly unfair trial and she is now a free woman. Before beginning my argument, I dedicated it to Morty's memory, and the eventual legal triumph was his last and perhaps most impressive monument.

For **M**orton **S**tavis

DECEMBER 18, 1992

I can't believe he never will be there

    If I just call him on the telephone;

I say, so deep inside: How could he dare

    To steal away and leave us all alone?

But then, I understand, he yet is here

    In everything we dream, and think, and do;

He's still a part of all that we hold dear,

    This man who fought the false and sought the true.

He was my colleague and my loving friend

    Who kept the system's devils from my door,

Who taught me that devotion knows no end

    And hopes that fail will one day rise and soar.

Try as I may, I cannot say goodbye

    To one of us who simply cannot die.

When Clarence Thomas was finally confirmed as an Associate Justice of the Supreme Court, I felt that we had finally scraped the very bottom of the barrel. I can only hope, without too much conviction, that the addition of Ruth Bader Ginsburg and Stephen Breyer to that bench will at least serve to moderate the more anti-libertarian leanings of that august body.

We now have Clarence Thomas on the Court

    To join the Gang of Five who want to bring

The Constitution's Bill of Rights up short

    And help resuscitate the British King.

Amendment by amendment, they've destroyed

    Two hundred years of legal precedent

As with our rights they've cavalierly destroyed

    And altered what the Founding Fathers meant.

Today, we've lost the freedoms that we'd earned

    At Trenton, Saratoga, and the rest

Of all those battles that, we once had learned,

    Were fought to culminate our righteous quest.

With justices like these, the die is cast

    That George the Third has really won at last.

During the Reagan-Bush years, hundreds of ultra-conservative judges, many of them woefully incompetent ideologues, were appointed to all levels of the federal courts. Nowhere was this more apparent than in the nomination of Supreme Court Justices, terminating with the horrendous selection of Clarence Thomas by President Bush. The additions of Antonin Scalia and Arthur Kennedy by President Reagan gave Chief Justice William Rehnquist the majority he needed to undo many of the gains of the civil rights struggles of the 1960's. One by one, this Gang of Five succeeded in invalidating much of the remedial legislation that had been gained at such cost in the streets of Birmingham, Alabama, and on the beaches of St. Augustine, to name but two of the more prominent battlegrounds. Even the valiant effort of the City Council of Richmond, Virginia, to insure that minority firms would be able to survive by guaranteeing them 30% of municipal contracts was overturned by the Gang of Five. Fortunately, Congress rolled back some of the more egregious decisions by enacting the Civil Rights Act of 1991.

The **S**upreme **C**ourt Majority

The Gang of Five who sit upon the Court

    Are bent on wiping out the Bill of Rights

As case by tragic case they sell us short,

    Extinguishing the Founding Father's lights.

They've overruled a Richmond statute meant

    To equalize the races by its terms

In ordering that triple ten percent

    Of city contracts go to black-owned firms.

They turned the clock back in a second case

    By making it impossible to end

Most racist treatment in the marketplace,

    Reversing what had been this nation's trend.

Controlled by each and every Reagan clone,

    This bench is now supreme in name alone.

Shortly after the country was shocked by the videotaped spectacle of Rodney King, a black man, being beaten and kicked by a squad of white Los Angeles police officers, a young Latino man in police custody in New York City suddenly died. The authorities maintained that his death was the result of his drug habit and not because he was brutalized by his captors, a traditional excuse in cases like this.

A **T**ale of **T**wo **C**ities

Los Angeles and New York's Borough of Queens

    Have much in common, it is sad to say;

Their police employ the self-same brutal means

    To terrorize their hapless Third World prey.

In L.A., they were caught on videotape—

    With clubs and kicks they broke a black man's bones,

And then excused the Constitution's rape

    By claiming that he merited his groans.

Three thousand miles directly to the east,

    Our Finest stopped a young Latino's breath,

And then proclaimed he was a drug-crazed beast

    Who quite deserved his violent early death.

In order to themselves exonerate,

    The cops now blame the victims for their fate.

There has been enough written about the hopelessness of the ghettos of our inner cities, the desperate existences led by the people forced to live there under the most onerous of conditions, and their chronic inability to climb the economic ladder. Yet, the white majority clings to the illusion that, in America, anyone who works hard and has the right attitude can easily get ahead. In his film, "Do the Right Thing," Spike Lee has the three elderly blacks, who serve as his Greek chorus, look at a neighborhood store recently opened by a Korean and ask the penetrating question, "Why can't we do that?" Of course, there is no easy answer to such a question, but it is not difficult to understand that terribly inferior schools, lack of jobs, families without fathers, proliferation of drugs, police brutality, and a racist criminal justice system contribute heavily to an inability to escape a debilitating environment. It is only in the prisons that blacks are permitted to have more than their proportionate share of the available cells, and they are also afforded greater representation with reference to capital punishment.

Their **S**hare of the Pie

For years, the blacks steadfastly have maintained

    That they have been denied an equal share

Of what their numbers should have surely gained

    For them if but the system had been fair.

To compensate for this disparity,

    We have made sure they have a higher rate

Of those who get the deadly penalty

    In each and every execution state.

To equalize the races even more,

    We give them greater numbers in our jails

And hope they know we've evened out the score

    By balancing the interracial scales.

Here in the USA, we do our best

    To see that every one is rightly blessed.

When President Bush named Clarence Thomas to replace the retiring Thurgood Marshall on the Supreme Court, many people were shocked by the utter hypocrisy of the nomination. Even Justice Marshall, when asked to comment about Bush's choice, was moved to comment that "A black snake is no better than a white one." Thomas was narrowly confirmed after barely surviving the accusations of Anita Hill that he had sexually propositioned her when they both worked at the Equal Employment Opportunity Commission (EEOC), he as its Executive Director and she as a staff attorney.

The Nomination of **C**larence **T**homas

The President has found his Judas goat,

    A black man with a soul of snowy hue,

Who knows just how to wear the bigot's coat

    And keep the poor from their God-given due.

He says minorities will need no aid

    To climb the ladder to a better day,

And everyone can join the big parade

    Without a friendly push along the way.

Self-help, he says, is all the people need

    To finally achieve equality,

And from discrimination to be freed

    In every blighted ghetto you can see.

As Thurgood said, in words not hardly trite,

    "A black snake is no better than a white."

The United Freedom Front, also known as the Ohio 7, was a group of white revolutionaries who believed in underground armed resistance. They were eventually charged with bombing certain military establishments in the New York area as well as a building owned by South African Airways. In every instance, adequate warnings were communicated to the targets in question in order to insure that no one was hurt when the bombs exploded. Their tactics were decried by the liberal establishment, but it was their conviction that peaceful protests were ineffective and that it was high time for violent action against property, not people. As one of their lawyers during their federal trial in Brooklyn, N.Y., I learned to respect their motives even though I thought their tactics were self-defeating.

United Freedom Front

The liberals decry the use of force

    To illustrate the evils of our age,

Maintaining that the only rightful course

    Is peaceful protest to express our rage.

Yet there are some who do not share that view

    And feel that they must turn a fiercer face

Upon the actions of the privileged few

    Who profit from the tyranny of race.

They place their bombs upon the property

    Of those whose products help the Bothas thrive,

But leave a warning for the world to see

    So that the many innocents survive.

Perhaps they represent the upraised fist

    Of men and women daring to resist.

On October 29, 1984, Eleanor Bumpurs, a 66-year-old emotionally disturbed black grandmother, resisted all efforts to evict her for nonpayment of rent from her Bronx apartment in a New York City housing project. When it became apparent that she would not voluntarily leave her home, the Emergency Services Unit police were called. After Sgt. Stephen Sullivan and five other white officers broke into her apartment, Ms. Bumpurs brandished a butter knife. Sullivan fired one blast from his shotgun, tearing off half of the hand that held the knife. He fired once more, this time causing her death. He was charged with manslaughter but elected to waive a jury and be tried by a white judge. On February 26, 1987, as expected, he was acquitted. In May of 1991, the city of New York agreed to pay Ms. Bumpurs' heirs $200,000.00 to settle their claims against it.

The **V**erdict

They didn't know how much she'd like to stay,

    Her home a little nearer to the sun,

And brought the police to pack her on her way,

    Eviction at the muzzle of a gun.

She couldn't understand she had to go

    Away from everything that she had known,

Or why the law had ruled it must be so

    That suddenly her fragile peace was flown.

She seized a knife and waved it at her foes,

    The only weapon that she could command;

The officer assumed a combat pose,

    His shotgun amputated half her hand.

The judge decided that it was no crime

    To shoot the woman down a second time.

This sonnet was written after the verdicts were rendered in the Yusef K. Hawkins case, the facts of which are set forth in the commentary to "In Memoriam I."

The juries sat for seemingly a year

    While all across the town, with bated breath,

Its residents were aching just to hear

    Who was responsible for Yusef's death.

At last, the Fama panel spoke its mind

    And found that wanton murder was his crime,

Which proved that justice is not always blind

    And whites who kill don't get off every time.

But then Mondello's jurors let him go

    Although he'd moved the actors on the stage

And ushered in this tragic tale of woe,

    A sorry verdict that turned joy to rage.

Strange, at the one who shot they threw the book

    But let the instigator off the hook.

By now, there cannot be anyone in the United States who has not been inundated by the media with all sorts of information, reliable or not, about the brutal murders of Nicole Brown Simpson and her friend, Ronald Goldman, on the night of June 12, 1994. Nicole's ex-husband, football icon O.J. Simpson, was charged with the double homicide. When I heard the news of his possible involvement in the two murders, I was struck with the paradox of how quickly a sports idol could be caught up in a tragedy of immense proportions. Of one thing I am certain, this will not be my last sonnet about the matter.

When the **C**heering **S**topped

O. J. SIMPSON—JUNE 1994

He once pranced through the opposition teams

    Whose lines would part like butter to the knife;

The press devoted countless newsprint reams

    To every fact of his collegiate life.

The Heisman Trophy soon became his prize

    And his initials known from West to East;

In Buffalo, he loved to hear the cries

    Of fans who gloried in each touchdown feast.

He then appeared upon the flickering screen

    To talk about the feats of other men;

His Hertz commercials showed him fit and lean,

    Still worthy of the news reporters' pen.

He's learned the cruellest lesson of them all—

    Celebrity does not prevent a fall.

In 1987, the State of New Jersey began a long criminal trial against Tommy Manning and Richard Williams, two members of a white revolutionary group, for the murder of one of its state troopers who had been killed in a shootout in Warren County. The two defendants were already serving federal prison terms which would insure that they would die in custody. During their trial in a reconverted garage in Somerville, N.J., they were represented by Lynne Stewart and myself. In addition to wondering why so much money was being expended in a case which could add nothing to their terms of imprisonment, we began to ask ourselves questions about comparative guilt in our society. It seemed passing strange that so much hatred could be levelled at our clients when our political and business leaders were not prosecuted for acts that seemed so much more heinous than the killing of a state trooper during a fire fight on a New Jersey highway.

Who Are the **G**uilty **O**nes?

They've spent a million dollars, maybe more,

    To demonstrate just how a trooper died,

While no one's ever prosecuted for

    The malformations of thalidomide.

They ring the courthouse with security

    To show the suspects are such evil men,

Yet thrill when we drop bombs on Tripoli

    Or send Marines to far-off Lebanon.

They pile the charges on them day by day

    So prison walls are all they'll ever see,

But those who rot their workers' lungs away

    Can use the law to save their treasury.

These are, alas, the very worst of times,

    When we excuse the very worst of crimes.

New York police officers who are accused of on-duty homicides always exercise their option of being tried by a judge alone, rather than by a jury. In every such instance, the trial judge turns out to be a Caucasian who promptly acquits the defendant. Because the officers know that this will be their fate if they are ever indicted, they are prone to fire their weapons without appropriate provocation.

Why **P**olice **O**fficers Often Kill

When policemen shoot to kill, there is a way

    To see to it that they stay in the clear—

They are supported by the PBA

    Which soon subjects each victim to a smear.

The DAs know that they must follow suit

    Or lose cooperation by the Force;

A quick grand jury is convened to moot

    The murder out by voting nay, of course.

When all too rarely cops are charged with crime,

    They understand from everything they've known

That they will never suffer prison time

    By opting for a trial by judge alone.

With such a background, it's not hard to see

    Why precinct trigger fingers are so free.

At the request of author James Baldwin and screen and television writer Abby Mann, I entered the case of Wayne Williams, the Georgia black who had been convicted of the murders of two adults in Atlanta but who was billed as the child murderer who had been killing young black children in that city in the early 1980s. Our legal team discovered that, during Wayne's high profile trial, his defense lawyers had never been furnished with materials that strongly indicated that the Ku Klux Klan was responsible for the murders in an effort to cause a race riot. In fact, the authorities had in their possession a report from a Klan infiltrator, whose services they had used for some eighteen years and who was considered extremely reliable, stating that he had heard a Klansman state that he intended to kill one Lubie Jeeter, who was indeed murdered a few weeks later. We filed a petition for a writ of habeas corpus which resulted in a number of evidentiary hearings fully documenting the withholding of crucial evidence which would have had a significant effect on the trial outcome if it had been made available to the defense. At this writing, the case is still pending.

There was no motive for this tiny man

    To massacre black children by the score,

Unless he followed some dark insane plan

    That brought a hidden impulse to the fore.

The police suspected who had stopped each life

    But thought it wiser that no one should know,

Afraid that truth would create racial strife

    And lead Atlanta to a greater woe.

So documents that proved some others' guilt

    Were buried deep in the official file,

While a perverted case was swiftly built

    By scientific puff and legal guile.

The Klan had ample reason to rejoice—

    The city's government had made its choice.

On February 27, 1973, a small band of Native Americans, led by members of the American Indian Movement (AIM), took over the small historic hamlet of Wounded Knee, S.D., the scene of the massacre of some 300 Minneconjou Sioux a few days after Christmas, 1890. The Indians remained in the village for seventy-one days in an effort to dramatize conditions on the Pine Ridge Reservation. For part of that time, I acted as chief negotiator for the occupiers, meeting every day in a nearby tipi with the representatives of the Department of Justice. On the twentieth anniversary, accompanied by my wife and two youngest daughters, I returned to Wounded Knee to join many of my old comrades in a remembrance of the occupation. We had a wonderful pipe ceremony near the common grave where the victims of the 1890 massacre were buried. Russell Means, who had just played a starring role in the film, "The Last of the Mohicans," and who had been one of the leaders of the occupation, led us in a memorial to two of our friends—Frank Clearwater and Buddy Lamont—who had been killed during the occupation and who were buried near those who had died in 1890.

Return to **W**ounded **K**nee

It's hard to comprehend it's twenty years

    Since first we came to Big Foot's captive land,

The chief a victim of his trail of tears,

    Along with all his Minneconjou band.

We stayed from February into May

    And gave the Great Sioux realm another birth;

We gathered near the common grave to pray

    For all who slept within our Mother Earth.

There is an awesome magic in this place

    That brings us back to here from everywhere

To find again somehow the inner grace

    That led us once to dream and hope and dare.

We try to seek, in paragraph or rhyme,

    A pathway through the corridors of time.

Emiliano Zapata, one of the leaders of the Mexican Revolution of 1910, was a champion of agrarian reform in his native state of Morelos. He steadfastly insisted that successive revolutionary governments abide by his 1911 Plan of Ayala, which called for the breakup of the giant sugar plantations in Morelos and the restoration of their lands to the state's Indian peasants. After collaborating with Pancho Villa in the capture of Mexico City in 1914, he returned to Morelos to continue his efforts to implement his Plan of Ayala. In 1919, he was lured by Venustiano Carranza, the President of Mexico, into an ambush and shot to death. Ironically, PRI, the governing party which emerged from the Revolution of 1910, has, for almost eight decades, dominated Mexican political life. As a result, a second Mexican Revolution began in the southern-most part of the country in 1994, when armed Indians, calling themselves Zapatistas, and seeking first class status, began to occupy a number of villages in the Chiapas region, until a temporary truce to await the outcome of the national elections in August was negotiated with the central government.

Emiliano **Z**apata

He strove against the haciendas' hold

    And for the pueblos' access to the land;

He learned the revolution had been sold

    To those who still maintained the privileged hand.

At first, he thought Madero was the one

    To bring about agrarian relief

And undo everything Diaz had done

    But hopeful trust soon changed to disbelief.

In Chimenaca, at the bugle's sound,

    The traitor's honor guard, at point-blank range,

Then fired twice and gunned him to the ground,

    As if one death could blunt the winds of change.

Would he have fought for land and liberty

    If he had known he paved the way for PRI?

Title Index